CONNECT *to* CLOSE

How to Communicate With Power, Build Momentum, and Drive Results

Amy Reczek

Thank you to my dad, who never missed an opportunity to make me feel special and taught me the value in the little moments in life.

TABLE OF CONTENTS

INTRODUCTION

What's the hardest part of selling?

It's not learning a CRM.

It's not placing X number of cold calls.

It's not understanding the buyer's journey.

It's not knowing when to follow up.

It's learning how to *communicate in a way that creates connection*—inside each of these pieces *and beyond them.*

Unfortunately, that's also the piece missing from most sales trainings, methods, and frameworks.

That's why placing those cold calls feels so hard.

That's why a voice in your head tells you that you're bothering prospects when you follow up.

That's why you get ghosted even when you do everything you're *trained to do.*

That's why you get burnt out and wonder if you're in the right career.

This isn't something that only happens to newbies. Even seasoned salespeople find themselves struggling.

The worst part is that we *know* this is happening. We know that old school sales tactics aren't enough anymore. We know that we need "soft skills." We know that we need to build relationships. Most of us have sat in trainings drilling that idea into our brains.

And still there's a missing piece of the puzzle. Even with all the training and the knowledge that we have at our fingertips about the "right" sales process and tactics, even with all the scripts we can find online, the overall sales close rate is *just 29%.*[1]

Why? Because connecting to close is about more than just listening, empathizing, or building relationships. Those things matter, but connecting in a way that moves your clients to action is different.

The truth is that anybody can build relationships. Anybody can shoot the shit with clients or have good conversations. Spending company dime taking teams to happy hours or golf outings may qualify as a decent relationship builder—but that isn't sales. The question is, are your conversations and relationships actually creating momentum?

This is something that I realized early on in my sales career. And the more I looked around, the more I realized that this momentum was what was lacking for so many salespeople, even great ones with years of experience. They were either sticking to old sales tactics or focusing so much on relationship building that they ended up in all fluff and no action mode, creating relationships that weren't leading to deals.

---

1 Phantom Team, "216 Statistics For Sales Reps In 2025," *PhantomBuster Blog,* October 11, 2024, https://phantombuster.com/blog/outbound-sales/sales-statistics/.

The problem is that nobody is teaching us how to build connection that moves deals forward. We receive plenty of training—hours and hours of it. But there's a gap in what we're learning.

Most trainings, conferences, team meetings, or sales books fall into one of three categories:

Problem #1: They offer the same recycled advice we've all heard before.

Problem #2: No substance. You can read the first chapter or two, and you've got it. And then you put down the book and never pick it up again because…what else is there to really say?

Problem #3: They're all theory, no action—great ideas on paper with zero direction on how to actually use them. They're too heavy on the *why* and way too light on the *how*. (Have you ever read a book or attended a conference that felt "life-changing," and then realized later that nothing actually changed? Yep, me too. Way too many to count.)

Many of these trainings and books have some great information in them. You need the basic sales know-how. You need relationship building to sell. Don't toss out what you've learned; it's the foundation you need. But you also need *more*.

Think about it like brewing a cup of coffee (stick with me for a minute here). Brew technically means "to bring about." And how do you bring about a cup of coffee? You pour water into a machine, add grounds or a pod, push a button, and out comes your coffee. That's how you think a cup of coffee is made. But inside the machine is a whole other world making it happen.

The water moves through the pipes. The heating element warms the water to the right temperature. Then, the water drips over the grounds, steeping for the ideal time period to perfectly extract the flavor.

And just like brewing a cup of coffee, brewing a sale takes a series of hidden steps. How we structure our meetings. The words we use. The way we communicate. Even how we hold our bodies. All of the overlooked pieces.

If we want to be more successful in sales, we can't just push the button. We have to learn how to be the machine that moves the sale along the way and brews the final result.

Here's the catch though. Nobody is teaching us how to do that. We're told we need the water, the filter, the coffee grounds (communication, confidence, empathy, etc.) However, we're not taught how any of them actually work.

The truth is that so-called soft skills are easy to acknowledge, hard to teach, and harder to implement. They can feel fluffy or woo-woo because nobody is teaching us the steps to put them together in a tangible way.

> **SOFT SKILLS ARE EASY TO ACKNOWLEDGE, HARD TO TEACH, AND HARDER TO IMPLEMENT.**

It's just assumed that we inherently know these things. They aren't treated like the learned skills that they are.

And when we feel like our sales process is stagnant or that something is missing, we don't know where to turn. Most managers aren't trainers. They're not taught how to work us through the soft skills or teach us to form better connections with clients.

That's what's missing in the corporate sales world.

We're told to play the numbers game, but we're not equipped with the modern sales skills we need to win.

We're told to "actively listen," but not taught about why it's so hard or how to start doing it differently.

We're told to build relationships but not taught how to move those relationships forward across the finish line.

We're told to empathize and listen but we're not given the tools to see what that practically looks like in action.

We're told to focus on value for our clients but aren't taught how to discover what that value is or how to actually communicate in a way that makes the client feel seen.

We're told to be confident but not given the techniques to actually raise our confidence.

And we're not given a space to ask questions, explore these ideas, or truly understand how to execute them in each phase of the sales process.

That's why this is NOT just another sales book. It's the book that's going to teach you how to truly connect with clients to create impact, fuel momentum, and move step by step to a close.

By the end of this book, you're going to know how to approach sales in a new way, using the power of moments to create real connection.

You'll learn how to get out of your own way, own the room, level up what you're already great at, build instant trust, and communicate in a way that makes people want to say YES.

At the end of the day, you are the expert. You're in your position for a reason. You have the baseline down. You know what you're doing. I'm not here to tell you that you have to reinvent yourself or toss out everything you're doing. I'm here to teach you how to make small shifts that can pave the way for more moments, more connection, and more closes.

Here's the framework of this book to get you there:

In part 1, you'll get the setup: what it really means to connect to close, how individual moments can change everything, and what sets powerful moments apart.

Then, in part 2, we will talk the BREW Method, a framework that shows you how to make moments, ignite opportunities, and connect with clients in a way that builds momentum. This includes everything from your physical presence to the way you *actually* "actively listen."

And as promised, in part 3, you'll get the *how*. You'll learn how to actively apply this in every phase of the sales process.

Finally, in part 4, you'll master how to hit the ground running, even if this approach feels new or uncomfortable.

The bottom line? Sales is evolving. Are you ready to evolve with it? You're in the right place.

If you're curious about where you or your team are at right now, and want to track your growth by the end of this book, head to SalesAndPresence.com/assessment to take the Connect to Close pre-assessment. It will evaluate how strong your connection skills are now and where you have room to grow. At the end of the book, you'll find a link to a post-assessment to track your progress after you implement everything you've learned.

Ready? Me too. Let's dive in.

—Amy

PART 1

See the Moment

CHAPTER 1

The Sales Evolution

Growing up, I was never the loudest kid in the room. I was the observer—the one quietly taking in everything around me.

While others were busy being heard, I was busy noticing. The expressions. The tone. The pauses between words. I was curious about people before I even knew that curiosity could become a career skill.

Ironically, I was also a theater and choir kid. I loved being on stage, performing, feeling the rhythm of an audience.

But even then, I wasn't chasing the spotlight; I was studying it. My performances captured everything I was observing about people—how they carried themselves, their body language, the way they used their voices. My curiosity also helped me tune into the audience: how they leaned in or didn't. What engaged them. What captivated them.

I didn't realize it at the time, but I was already learning presence—how energy, tone, and timing can shift a room. I was building the skills that I eventually turned to when I landed my first sales job.

I didn't have a background in business or a stack of playbooks to follow. I had no idea what "pipeline" even meant. What I did have was the same curiosity I'd always had, the same instinct to watch, listen, and learn.

I wasn't interested in being the loudest person in the room; I was interested in being the one who *understood the room.*

And it worked. I listened more than I talked. I connected easily and built strong relationships. People trusted me, and I began to climb. But as it turns out, I was still missing a big piece of the sales puzzle, and it took a misstep for me to realize it.

I had a longtime client who felt more like a friend. Every quarter, I'd call him to set up a meeting, travel out to visit the office, check in, answer any questions, and pitch a new service if we had something to offer. Then I'd take the team out for happy hour.

Sound familiar? Yep, it's what every great relationship-building salesperson does. I was doing everything "right," at least by traditional sales standards.

Every so often, though, he'd mention Tony, my competitor.

"Tony stopped by again," he'd say. "He showed us how one change in our system could improve results." I brushed it off. Tony might have lived nearby, but I had the relationship. Surely that was stronger.

Until one day, the relationship wasn't enough.

Seven years in, the invoices stopped.

I called to see what happened. My client hesitated, then said the words no salesperson ever wants to hear: "Amy…I went with Tony."

Was my relationship building on point? Yep. I had built such a strong relationship that my client felt bad admitting to me that he was moving to a different company. We're still Facebook friends to this day.

But what I had missed was that Tony was coming in and not just building a relationship, but also building credibility. He was engaging with my client in a different way. He was looking beyond the product (essentially the exact same thing I sold) and listening to what my client needed, explaining how he could help, and demonstrating it for my client.

That's credibility. That's how you build trust. That's how you connect to close. Tony was making moments with my client— moments that proved he understood my client, valued him, and could help strengthen his business. Could I have done the same? Yes. Did I completely miss it? Yes.

That's when I realized that relationship-building alone isn't enough. We need real *connection*. The future of sales belongs to those who can communicate in a way that conveys credibility and establishes trust, creating impact and building momentum, moment by moment.

That's the new equation. That's connecting to close.

Sales has evolved. Buyers are more informed, markets are noisier, and attention is harder to earn. To keep closing, we have to evolve too.

Why the Shift in Sales?

What comes to mind when you think of a salesperson?

If your answer was something like pushy, used car salesman, or sleazy, you're not alone.

What's really interesting is that almost everyone (even seasoned salespeople) gives this answer.

Here's some fun science for you: as part of the book *To Sell is Human*, Daniel Pink conducted a study with 5,000 people. The number one word associated with the idea of a salesperson is "pushy," and the image was a sleazy used car salesman in a polyester suit.[2]

This is the idea that has stuck.

And here's the thing: how many actual people in B2B sales do you know who fit the pushy used car salesman stereotype? Probably one at most. Maybe none.

If you're reading this book, investing in your growth, and taking sales seriously? *You're definitely not that person.*

So why is the image so strong?

Because we've been conditioned to believe that sales is intrusive, that we're bothering the client instead of bringing value to them.

---

2   Pink, Daniel H., *To Sell Is Human: The Surprising Truth About Moving Others* (Riverhead Books, 2012).

That's not how sales works now. And it's definitely not where we're going in the future.

Sales as we know it took shape in the corporate world of the 1990s. Back then, the structure of American business shaped a rigid, old-school approach, one that was built for a different time, a different customer, and a different level of access to information.

As we all know, the world has changed. Technology has shifted the way people buy, the way they interact, and the way they make decisions. Clients have more choices. They're more skeptical. They're not just buying a product anymore. They're buying the person behind it. The brand that backs it. The values it represents. And most of all, the trust it builds.

We've had to keep up with a lot of changes as technology has advanced. And then came COVID, and with it, change on a level we never anticipated. In many ways, we're *still* figuring it out. The pandemic transformed the way we sold. Before that, we already "knew" we should make video content and add it to our emails or put a nice photo in our signature. And most of us simply weren't doing it. Once COVID hit, we had to change the way we met, the way we connected, and the way we communicated. It showed us how important it was to connect visually, and made those virtual visuals even more important.

AI is another example. If you're like many salespeople, you're either terrified that it's going to take your job or you think it's the magic button that's going to solve all of your problems. The reality check? It's neither. AI is a tool, just like your CRM or all the other systems that help you succeed. It can streamline our work and make us a hundred times more productive. And at the same time, it doesn't replace us. In fact, it makes it even more important to learn how to communicate and connect.

Even with all the change that's reshaped business—technology, automation, virtual everything—the *core* of sales hasn't changed. It still starts and ends with trust and connection.

What has changed is how much harder that trust is to earn. With endless tools, platforms, and AI in the mix, it's easy to lose the very thing that makes selling human.

So how do you stand out? You focus on the experience you create for your clients, moment by moment.

> **FOCUS ON THE EXPERIENCE YOU CREATE FOR YOUR CLIENTS, MOMENT BY MOMENT.**

That's the piece that's missing in most sales training. It's not what's being taught in onboarding decks or product demos. But it's what actually moves deals forward.

And that's the journey you're about to take.

Maybe you're reading this book because your boss told you to.

Maybe a colleague recommended it.

Maybe you're an executive looking for a fresh way to inspire your team.

Or maybe you've been in sales for decades and think you already know it all. Have you evolved over those decades? Guess what? Clients and sales have too.

No matter what brings you here, my promise to you is this: your time is not going to be wasted—every word is here for a reason. And if you take the BREW Method and apply it, it *will* make a difference.

Here's what you can expect:

- Honest conversations
- Science and proof that back up the ideas you'll learn
- Stories—plenty of them. Especially coffee stories
- Quick action tips you can implement right away (I call them "Espresso Shots")

And here's my ask of you:

- Be open and curious.
- Be willing to show up differently and get a bit uncomfortable.
- Take action; put the Espresso Shots into play.

I want to be clear, the ideas you're going to learn are anything but "soft." They're powerful. They're game-changing. And they're hard to do—especially at first.

My number one piece of advice? Just do it.

Nike nailed it back in 1988; not just because it sounded good, but because it captured something real. Their message wasn't about the gear; it was about the grind. They were there with you when you laced up for that early morning run, when it was pouring rain, and when you didn't feel like doing the work. One foot in front of the other. That's how progress happens.

That's exactly what it takes to build the skills you're about to learn. Just do it, and know I'm right here with you.

Do the work. Be open. INVEST IN YOU.

Some of the skills will feel new. Some will deepen ideas you have already heard and give you the missing piece you need to put them into play. Some of it will be quick wins that you can incorporate right away. Some of it will be deeper work.

I want you to know that everything you learn and every change you make can have an **INVEST IN YOU.** impact on how you show up, the relationships you build with your clients, and the connection and communication you have.

And to understand *why*, let's think about brewing a good cup of coffee together.

I have a thing for coffee. And I'm not alone—people in the United States consume 400 million cups of coffee daily.[3] Coffee is having a moment. It isn't just a drink; it's a whole vibe.

What makes coffee so special?

It's not the caffeine. It's all about *the moments*.

It's the smell that brings you back to childhood, waking up in a house where coffee was always brewing.

It's sitting in a coffee shop, surrounded by strangers, feeling a quiet sense of community.

It's the ritual, whether it's a pour-over that takes twenty meticulous minutes (NOT me, although I love your patience if this is you), a jolt from an espresso machine (holy caffeine hit) or a quick-and-easy cup from a pod (yep, this one's me. I have no patience).

---

3   James Bellis, "Coffee Consumption Statistics US (Charts & Infographics)," *Balance Coffee*, October 12, 2025, https://balancecoffee.co.uk/blogs/blog/coffee-consumption-statistics-us.

For so many of us, coffee is a moment we give ourselves. When I'm on the road for work, the very first thing I do in the morning? Order room service. Not for the food—let's be real—it's all about the coffee.

Sure, I could settle for whatever sad excuse for coffee they've left in the hotel room. But that would be a very different experience.

First, the coffee? Undrinkable.

Second, the coffee maker? Questionable at best, a health hazard at worst.

And let's not even get started on the water situation. Unless I've got my own bottled water on hand, that's a hard nope from me.

It's not just about coffee. Maybe you have tea. Maybe you have Diet Coke or lemon water. The point is that we all have rituals, routines, and moments we hold dear.

To brew a cup of coffee or tea means to follow a set of steps and then step back and let the flavor gradually form and become potent. It takes a process. It takes time. It takes intention.

And sales? It's the same.

The way you connect to close is by creating *moments that brew into something more*. That's where the idea for the BREW Method was born. That's where we're heading.

CHAPTER 2

The Power of a Moment

Picture an ordinary, busy day for you. You have a big project at work that you need to get to and there's an impending deadline.

You wake up and check your email before you've even gotten out of bed. While you eat breakfast, you respond to a few messages.

You brush your teeth, your mind jumping ahead to what you need to get done as soon as you get to work—the emails you need to respond to, the contracts you need to write, the meetings you have on your schedule, and everything you need to do to prepare.

In the car, you put on a self-help podcast, multitasking, because let's face it, you're the master of that.

You stop for coffee on the way to work. Because honestly, you didn't think this story would unfold without coffee, did you? You're a badass with an app so of course you order ahead and pick it up through the drive-thru. Seriously, who has time to actually walk in?!

The barista hands you your order and you mumble a quick, "Thanks" before you drive off.

When you get to work, you move quickly to your desk, set down your coffee, and start putting all the pieces you thought about into motion.

Sounds like a productive morning, right?

What did you miss?

How were the people in your home doing this morning? If you have a partner, kids, or a pet? What was going on for them? Was there a relaxed, connected moment? Or was it all rush, rush, rush?

What did the sky look like? Was there a sunrise? A rainbow? A cloud that reminded you of anything?

At the coffee shop, how old was the barista? What color was their hair? What was their name? How did they seem to be doing? Stressed? Excited? Friendly?

When you walked into the office and headed to your desk, did you notice anyone around you? Did you connect with anyone? Who was nearby? What were they doing? Or, if you work from home, did you check in with anyone on your team? How did they seem?

If you're like most people, the answer to a lot (if not all) of these questions is, "I don't know," because you rushed through everything. You looked at your phone. You focused more on what was in your own head than what was going on around you.

I'll ask you again, how many moments did you miss?

Maybe your kid or your partner wanted to tell you something, and you didn't take the time to slow down and listen.

Maybe someone in your family was nervous about something, and you were distracted and missed the chance to connect and offer support.

Maybe someone in the line at Starbucks was holding a book you would have loved—a book you'll never even know about because you weren't noticing.

Maybe the barista would have said something that would make your day and lift you up. Since you were closed off, they stuck to the task at hand instead of engaging in conversation.

Maybe someone else in the coffee shop was a person you used to know or someone who had a shared interest you could have talked about. Or maybe one of them was even a potential client or a valuable connection. Maybe they had career advice or an "in" at a dream job.

The sad part is, you'll never know. Those moments are gone. You missed them, just like that.

You've been conditioned to operate this way. To be "productive." To multi-task. To get more done. To live in your head. To pick up your phone at every lull in activity (I mean, really, when was the last time you were away from your phone for 5 minutes?). To completely miss the moments around you.

As you go about your day, without even realizing it, you're on autopilot. Pack bags. Check texts. Drive to work. Get in, get out. Fast. Efficient. And *empty.*

We're not noticing what's happening. We're not tuned into the world around us.

My husband and I were recently sitting at home working when out of nowhere we heard a loud crash. We rushed to the window to look outside—and saw a teenager on an e-bike who had run straight into the back of my husband's car. Why? She was on her phone.

Luckily she was wearing a helmet, and she wasn't hurt. She was shaken up; we went out to check on her and she barely stopped herself from bursting into tears. The situation could have been much worse…and it all stemmed from not being able to disconnect long enough for a bike ride with her friends.

And she's hardly an exception. Even when people aren't on their phones, they're often distracted, caught up in their heads instead of paying attention to the moment around them.

What does all this have to do with sales? EVERYTHING.

How many meetings have you sat in where you were thinking of everything but the meeting? How many client interactions have you had where you asked a question and didn't hear a

> **86% OF CLIENTS STATE THAT THE EXPERIENCE THEY HAVE IS JUST AS IMPORTANT AS THE PRODUCT OR SERVICE THEY BUY.**

word they said in response because you were so focused on the next thing you were going to say?

Every moment is a chance to connect. To create. To solve. To become a partner. To create an *experience.* And that's what clients want now. In surveys, 86% of clients stated that the experience they have is just as important as the product or service they buy.[4]

The question is, how do you create a memorable experience? You listen. You stay curious. You stay present. You create moments that build into an experience worth having.

Moments that Matter

My dad was a moment maker. He was the one driving me to sports, voice lessons, and every activity in between—and he always made sure the little moments counted.

Every now and then after school, we'd hit up this tiny, hole-in-the-wall donut shop. I always got the same donut. He always got a cup of coffee. (Looking back, that was probably my first clue that coffee would be a lifelong obsession.)

We were a baseball family. Our town had a Cincinnati Reds farm team just down the street, and I practically grew up at that ballpark. Every game, same spot on the bleachers. I even ended up singing the national anthem for some of the games throughout high school. My dad taught me the game play by play, quizzing me on what just happened or breaking down a call so I could understand it.

When the team was on the road, we had our own tradition: Hardee's drive-thru for a vanilla ice cream cone, then straight to our VIP parking spot behind the field (a side street) to listen to the Yankees on the radio. Our own version of box seats.

---

4 "Genesys Study Reveals Companies are Missing the Mark on Customer Experience," Genesys, April 5, 2023, https://www.genesys.com/company/newsroom/announcements/122891

And Christmas? Oh, that was a whole production. The tree had to be just right: either blue and silver or red and gold, no exceptions. Christmas Eve? Always the same fancy dinner at a historic downtown hotel.

He was the dad who purposely created moments. He didn't just leave Post-it notes in my lunchbox; he took the time to write little reminders that I was loved and capable, all designed to lift me up.

He had this mindset of creating moments that made people feel safe, seen, and special. Every interaction, every gesture was thought out and intentional.

And that's exactly how you should approach your clients. Think about it—what better way is there to craft an experience they'll remember? One that builds trust, makes them feel valued, and keeps them coming back for more?

When you start becoming the moment maker for your clients, you're opening the door for stronger, more meaningful connections. And that's where the real magic happens.

Shifting the Mindset to Moments

How do you become the moment maker? First, let's talk about how you *don't*.

How many times have you spoken to a salesperson who clearly just was *not* listening to you? They were already prepared with their next response, no matter what you said. How did it feel? I'm guessing shitty and annoyed…not special, right?

That's what happens when you focus on the sale, the close, or the next thing that you're "supposed to say." It's what happens when you stick to a sales process even when pieces of it feel inauthentic. It's what happens when you don't show up as yourself or actually listen to the people in front of you. You miss the moments, just like you do when you're moving through your morning without slowing down and pausing to look around.

The traditional approach to sales trains you to do this. The Elevator pitch. Sales processes. Ways to move the person you're talking to along the funnel to a purchase. These things aren't "bad" but they do need an update. And that update starts with a mindset shift about "goals."

I talked to someone at a recent sales training who told me that he was finding conferences unsuccessful for him.

I asked him, "Well, what is it that you're trying to do?"

And he said what so many people (possibly you) would say. "To get business."

Nope. That's where we go wrong. We focus on the overall goal instead of the intention of the moment in front of us. Getting business, your big sales goal, is *the result* of all the moments added up together. Your intention is where to put your focus *in that moment*; in this case, to introduce yourself with impact and get to the next meeting. In his book *Atomic Habits*, James Clear writes, "You do not rise to the level of your goals. You fall to the level of your systems."[5] In other words, your goals are not

---

5   Clear, James. Atomic Habits: An Easy & Proven Way to Build Good Habits & Break Bad Ones. New York: Avery, 2018.

what create your success—your systems are. And connecting to close is about building a system of moments that work together and committing fully to each of those moments.

Think of it like dating. You're not trying to propose on the first date. You're hoping to get to know someone and hopefully get a second date. You're layering momentum step by step.

When you focus on the intention of a moment instead of the big goal, it becomes easier to show up like a human being and not get in your own way by coming on too strong or not strong enough.

For example, someone recently told me about how they'd made a potential business connection at a party over the weekend.

When I asked him what his next step was, he said, "Well, I'll probably wait a week or two and follow up."

Let's jump back to the dating metaphor. If you met someone that you were interested in and they waited two weeks before they even contacted you again, how would you feel? Would you take the call? That moment of connection would be gone, and you'd probably have moved on to someone else.

That's why it's so important to have the right intention in mind. When you focus on the sale, you do things that don't make sense. You try to close right away. You send your whole sales spiel over DM without even knowing someone. Or you wait too long to reach out. Or you show up without confidence because you think of yourself as a burden. Or you rush past moments. You get in your own way.

As you move forward, remember your intention. It's not to make a sale. It's to make a moment that matters, that *ultimately brews into the sale*. There are a lot of ways to do this, and we'll cover many of them throughout this book.

For now, though, there is one important place to start…being *in* the moment.

You can't brew moments that turn into something more powerful later without being able to see the moment around you and actually be *in* it.

There's something powerful, even revolutionary, about learning how to stop, be still, and observe what's around you without thinking ahead or behind.

In their book, *Two Beats Ahead: What Musical Minds Teach Us About Innovation*, authors Panos A. Panay and R. Michael Hendrix give their readers a fascinating look at how thinking like a musician ties into business and entrepreneurship. One particularly interesting idea has to do with a rest, also known as the pause between the notes.

These authors point out that it's often the spaces, the pauses, that actually draw us into the music or evoke our emotions.[6] Similarly, in a conversation, it's pausing, observing what's going on, what's being said, and what's *not* being said that gives you insight that you will never get if you are too busy in your own head instead of being in the moment.

That's your starting point.

---

6   Panos A. Panay and R. Michael Hendrix, *Two Beats Ahead: What Musical Minds Teach Us About Innovation*, (PublicAffairs, 2021).

Espresso Shot: Your Challenge

Things you can do right now to start showing up differently in the way you interact with people:

- The next time you're in a coffee shop or a restaurant, put down your phone and look around you. Notice something about three different people. Sit in awareness.
- Strike up a conversation this week with someone—a neighbor or a stranger.
- Create a moment for yourself today, whether it's coffee-related or stepping outside going for a walk or just sitting and being in the moment. Notice how it makes you feel.

CHAPTER 3

What Sets Certain Moments Apart?

If I asked you to tell me every single thing you did yesterday, moment by moment, could you? You probably couldn't remember every moment, but you could piece it together for the most part. But what about a week ago? Or two weeks? By then, most of the moments that you experienced are gone.

There are a lot of moments in a day, but how many really stick? Not most of them.

In 1885, German psychologist Hermann Ebbinghaus developed "The Forgetting Curve" based on research he conducted to measure memory. It charts the amount of details people forget after a certain amount of time. His results showed that within 20 minutes of learning something, we forget 40% of it. By the end of the day, most of it's gone. And a month later, we only remember 20%.[7] And that was measuring something people *were actively trying to learn and remember.*

---

7 "Forgetting Curve," ScienceDirect Topics, accessed April 4, 2025, https://www. sciencedirect.com/topics/agricultural-and-biological-sciences/forgetting-curve.

How much harder is it to remember day-to-day interactions?

Think about moments in your career that stand out to you. You likely remember the big moments—promotions, big changes, maybe the largest contract you executed.

You also probably remember the negative ones—rough interactions or moments where you feel like you failed.

I can remember some of the best cups of coffee I've ever had. And I can also remember the worst ones. (The best cups of coffee are those generated in a moment that you love. The worst ones seem to always be from a hotel room or a gas station.)

But what about the everyday moments? The ones that aren't huge or life changing? The ones that aren't negative? The ones that stick with you even if you're not quite sure why? Even in the big moments, the little everyday moments *within it* have the most impact.

Think about moments like that. What comes to mind? Maybe a great interaction with a co-worker? Maybe a client who felt like an instant friend? Maybe a word of recognition from a supervisor?

Your job is to make those types of moments for your clients— little moments with big impact.

Maybe you notice a photo on a client's desk of a vacation that leads to a connection about somewhere you've both traveled, or one of you has a dog that pops into the Zoom call and spurs a conversation about how much you both love animals. (I can't tell you how many clients have met my miniature poodle over Zoom and how many dogs I have virtually met). Amazing.

In sales, an example of a moment that matters can be:

- Having a killer first impression that lasts
- Entering a room with complete confidence
- Learning something new and valuable about your client
- Ending a meeting with a crystal clear call to action
- Carefully choosing the words you say to leave the biggest impact
- Developing a follow-up cadence that offers value to the client
- Staying curious and engaging in the moment
- Listening to what the client is *not saying* and being able to articulate their needs before they have even verbalized them
- Having open posture that invites your client to trust you
- Noticing that a client is having an off day and taking the time to ask why
- Leaving a cold voicemail that doesn't feel like a waste of your client's time
- Leading a conversation with a clear plan while also connecting like a human being
- Having a great conversation at a conference with someone you didn't know

None of those moments seem mystical or out of reach, right? Individually, they can even seem insignificant. But together, they *create an experience.*

When you take a series of moments like these, executed with confidence, openness, and curiosity, you stand out. You convey leadership. You leave an impact. You brew momentum, moment by moment.

Becoming a Moment Maker

When I think back to the moments my dad made, and *why* they stood out, a few themes pop up:

They were repeated. If he had taken me to a donut shop one time, would I remember it? Maybe, maybe not. The routine we had is what stood out. The consistent smell of his

CONSISTENCY MATTERS.

coffee, the taste of the donut—those details only stick around because it's something we did again and again. Repetition sticks. Consistency matters.

They were out of the ordinary. Even though those moments were things we did over and over, they were still outside of the mundane. They weren't things that happened every single day. They were special.

They were built on connection. These moments were shared. They were part of our connection, part of our relationship.

They were intentional. My dad made these moments with intention. Was his intention for me to remember them forever and to train people to make moments? No. His intention was to create something special for me in those individual moments. The same applies to being a moment maker in sales. Your intention isn't to close the deal. It's to make an experience for your client.

I know you've heard that advice before. Be more intentional. Listen more. I get it—it's not a shocker. And at the same time, how often have you heard it, said you were going to do it, and then…nothing changed? Or is it something you think about but don't know how to put into play? It *is* obvious. It isn't *easy*. If it was, everyone would be doing it. They're not. This is rare. And when it does happen, it stands out. It makes an impact.

And if you can learn how to do it, you're going to be memorable. You're going to build trust. You're going to make moments that create an experience.

Let's think back to the Forgetting Curve from the beginning of this chapter. There's a reason why things fade away over time. We aren't supposed to remember everything. Our brains make space for new learning and prepare us for the most important tasks by removing less important information.

The question is, are you going to be part of the 80% of interactions that fade away for your potential clients? Or are you going to stay in the 20% that stick?

CHAPTER 4

Real-Life Moments That Resonated

Talking about making moments in theory is one thing, but what does it look like in action?

In this chapter, we're going to explore three stories of standout moments that resonated with me and why. From there, we'll learn how to start brewing these types of moments in sales.

Each of these moments has a lot of different pieces to it—the body language people showed up with, the way they listened and spoke, the connection points made along the way. Every moment has dozens of little facets that make it resonate.

All of those facets are worth paying attention to. And at the same time, I know that if you try to remember everything, you'll likely lose steam and end up not making the progress you want to make.

Let's not do it that way. Before you go any further in this book, take out a piece of paper or start a note on your phone and add this title: *My Power Three*.

As you read the stories, learn the frameworks, and reflect on your own habits, certain ideas will jump off the page. Some concepts probably hit you with a jolt of recognition, an "aha" moment, or maybe even a twinge of "oof, I really need to work on that."

When that happens, add it to your note. By the end of the book, you're going to have a lot to reflect on and think about, and I don't want you to walk away so overwhelmed that you don't put anything into action.

That's where your Power Three will come in. From a psychology standpoint, the human brain can only handle a few new things at a time. Three is going to be your magic number to give you a starting point to work on.

At the end, you are going to look back at your takeaways and break this down to the three most important ideas you learned along the way. These are areas where you can make the biggest difference for yourself. This will create your starting point as you wrap up the book.

Moment 1: Starbucks Kid

It's no surprise that my first story starts in a Starbucks—coffee shops are full of coffee and people. They're a prime spot to make, or miss, moments.

I had traveled to LA for a training for a new client I hadn't met in person before. It was a big day. I got up early in the morning so I could walk to Starbucks to get a coffee to start my day (it's a superpower of mine to have a coffee in hand when I walk into a client's office. It tells them something about my personality, it gives me something to do with my hands that keeps me open physically, and it's a great conversation starter if they are also a coffee person).

When I walked into Starbucks, someone greeted me immediately.

"Hello! Good morning." He was standing in front of the counter greeting people…so at first, I didn't know that he was an employee there.

"Good morning!" I responded and got in line to order.

After I ordered, I moved over to wait for my coffee. That's when I realized that he was the person who called out names when the orders were ready.

In between orders coming up, he was also engaging in conversation with everyone waiting. When I was next in line, he asked me what I did. I told him and his eyes lit up.

It turned out that he was a business major at a local college. While we waited for my coffee, he asked me dozens of questions about owning a business, how to get into a business, and what he should do to be successful.

My coffee came up and he handed it to me and said, "Have a great day! Thanks for the conversation."

It completely made my day. I walked out of there, coffee in hand, thinking, "I got this. This training is going to be awesome." And it was all because of him, his engagement, and that interaction that stood out.

Why Did It Resonate?

Here are all the things Starbucks Kid did that made the moment stand out:

- He removed the barrier: Instead of standing behind the counter (a physical barrier separating him from everyone else), he stood in front of it.
- He was intentional, going above and beyond to make everyone feel seen.
- He made eye contact: This nonverbal communication showed interest and created connection. (We'll talk more about nonverbal communication in part 2.)
- He greeted everyone immediately, then re-engaged with every person and asked specific questions about THEM.
- He ended the interaction positively.

What if he hadn't done these things? I wouldn't have had the same bounce in my step leaving Starbucks…and *he* also would have missed out on the chance to get some business insight. Instead, he formed this powerful moment that stood out to me so much that I'm sharing it with you now.

Nothing he did was revolutionary. Everything he did was intentional. And there are plenty of sales lessons in the interaction:

- Remove the barrier: Barriers keep us closed off from people. In business, the barrier is a desk or a booth at a conference—take a page from Starbucks Kid's book and remove that barrier by standing in front of it instead of staying behind it.

- Engage differently: Be the first to say hello and be the first to be curious.
- Ask questions: Starbucks Kid was "you framing" (putting the focus on the other person), probably without realizing what it was. We'll dive more into this concept in part 2, but the lesson here is to put the focus on your client instead of on you and your pitch.
- End strongly and positively: Close out every interaction with a genuine, kind moment. In sales, this also means a CTA (call to action…or as I like to call it *confidence to act*—confidently and clearly pointing to the next step).

The Flip Side

Just two weeks after my great interaction with Starbucks Kid, I stood in another Starbucks, at the airport in a different state.

I had pre-ordered my coffee this time—I was about to drive an hour and needed a caffeine boost.

When I walked in, the barista was standing behind the counter chatting with some friends. She didn't greet me or even look up at me.

My coffee was ready, sitting on the counter. I grabbed it and looked around for a straw, unable to find one.

I waited, and finally, the barista looked over at me, clearly annoyed. Her body language was fully closed off; she didn't turn her body toward mine or even say anything to me.

I said, "I'm looking for a straw; can you tell me where they are?"

Without saying a word, she pointed to where the straws were, then rolled her eyes and turned back to her friends.

Do you think I walked out of *that* Starbucks feeling ready to take on the world? Far from it. I had to intentionally reset to not let that interaction ruin my day.

It was so different from my other Starbucks Kid story. I remember it for all the wrong reasons. And for her, that moment was nothing. If *she* was a business major, she definitely didn't get any advice from me. She closed herself off from anyone who might be walking in, missing every chance to make a moment.

Whatever you do, don't be like *that* Starbucks Kid. Be like the first one.

Moment 2: The Elevator Secret Identity

My next story takes place in an elevator, but it actually starts as I was leaving a hotel room heading down to the conference, before I even got to the elevator.

Pro tip: your meeting (or conference or event) starts *before* you walk into the room. Normally, from the second I step out of my hotel room, I'm mentally ready, open, and looking around with curiosity (nothing in my hands, open posture, eyes alert).

YOUR MEETING (OR CONFERENCE OR EVENT) STARTS BEFORE YOU WALK INTO THE ROOM.

On this day, though, I was momentarily on my phone, figuring out directions. As always, I was hyper-aware of my surroundings so that I wouldn't miss opportunities to engage and connect with the people around me. So when the elevator doors opened and revealed a gentleman inside, I immediately put away my phone.

I noticed he was wearing a lanyard. Perfect—I'd just follow him to the event.

We started chatting about the upcoming conference, having a great conversation. We got off the elevator and walked to the room together.

When we got there, he shook my hand warmly and said, "Great talking with you. I assume you're our speaker today. I'm the CEO of the company."

Pause and rewind. CEOs don't usually hire me. That's HR, marketing, or sales. This was a *moment* without a doubt.

I had no idea who he was. No idea I was secretly chatting with the CEO. No idea how important the moment would be.

And it happened because I was open and engaged.

How often do you scroll on your phone in the elevator or just smile and nod as you get on only to stay in your head? If I had stayed focused on my phone, I would have missed the moment. Instead, I made a meaningful connection.

Why Did It Resonate?

Here's exactly what made this elevator moment powerful:

1. I put the phone away so I could instantly engage. Phones are conversation killers. Don't let them sabotage your moments.

2. I kept my posture open. We're going to dive deep into posture and nonverbal communication later in the book. For now, think of posture like primate behavior (seriously). Strong posture signals confidence and openness and invites engagement. We're hardwired to respond positively to this.

3. My hands were welcoming. Hands are major trust builders. Subconsciously, they're one of the first things people notice. Open hands signal safety—no hidden threats here.

The Flip Side

A few months before, at a different conference, I had another elevator encounter. This one stood out because of the moment missed by someone I shared the elevator with.

That day, I knew where I was going. I left my hotel room, open and ready to engage with anyone. A woman joined me at the elevator, and we exchanged friendly "good mornings."

As we stepped inside, she asked, "What floor?"

"One," I said. "I'm headed straight for coffee."

She laughed, agreeing, "Me too. I need coffee."

Coffee talk? She was basically already my best friend.

"What's your coffee drink of choice?" I asked.

She answered, and before I could even respond, she had already buried herself in her phone.

Just like that, she slipped into "low-power mode": closed off, unapproachable, conversation completely done.

Here's the kicker: I was the keynote speaker for her event, with over 900 people attending. It would have been a safe assumption that I was one of the 900 attendees. I could've been a CEO, a client, or (hello!) the speaker. She missed the moment. She had the chance to engage, build rapport, or simply have a memorable interaction, and it passed her by.

Moment 3: Witnessed It in Real Time

My third story takes place in Dallas, as I headed out for the post-learning cocktail hour after training a room full of corporate professionals about moments, experiences, and connecting to close.

I was in the back of the elevator watching several of the conference attendees file in (every great story somehow begins in an elevator). They were all dressed ready to go out, in professional attire, chatting with each other excitedly.

Another woman, clearly headed to the gym in workout gear, stepped onto our packed elevator.

Instead of quietly facing the doors, she hesitated, smiled, and made eye contact.

"Well, you all look much fancier than me!" she joked. The ice broke instantly. Everyone laughed, chimed in, and genuinely enjoyed that shared minute.

When she got off, she turned around, waved warmly, and wished everyone a great evening.

The moment she left, one woman in our group turned to her colleagues and said, "That right there was the experience Amy was talking about!"

Ironically, she didn't even realize I was standing right behind her.

Someone said, "Well, Amy's in here!"

The woman who had pointed out the experience turned, laughed, and said, "Did you *plant* her for this?"

(Spoiler: I didn't—but note to self, brilliant idea for the future.)

I talk about moments and experiences constantly, but seeing it organically happen in real time was extraordinary.

Why Did It Resonate?

Here's what made that elevator interaction stand out:

- Every single person was present, creating an open atmosphere.
- Gym Lady engaged immediately—she didn't close herself off from the group she wasn't a part of.
- Gym Lady also stayed curious. She looked around and smiled, joked, and interacted.
- She created a memorable ending. She made eye contact, turned towards the group, and closed the interaction positively.

The Flip Side

The flip side here could be any moment you're in an elevator. We've all experienced this after long-winded conferences. What usually happens?

- Everyone is closed off or on their phones
- People only talk when asking someone, "What floor?"
- Nobody takes notice of each other.
- If someone comes in that's not part of the group, they stay closed off right away.

It's something we've all seen time and time again.

Wrapping It Up: This Is Your Moment

The three moments I picked weren't specifically sales related. Why? This isn't *Severance* (but it's a great fucking show). Who we are in our personal lives and who we are in business is connected. There is no clean divide between your professional self and your personal self.

If you can become an authentic moment maker at home or out and about in your life, you're going to be able to put this into practice at work. In fact, the moments we have outside of work are often the best place to start.

Now, I want to be clear that you don't have to go around in your life always being "on." You don't have to be making moments every second of every day. It's completely unrealistic, not to mention *exhausting*.

Sometimes you don't *want* to make a moment. Own that. It's fine. You're not going to make moments *all the time*, even at work. If you're at the airport about to return home, burnt out from travel, and you just don't want to engage with anyone, cool. Pop on your headphones and give *yourself* a moment.

(I would argue that you still need to maintain some level of awareness of your surroundings. At an icebreaker recently, one of the attendees shared that he walked straight into a wall while he was scrolling Instagram. We all got a great laugh out of it—and it's also something we all want to avoid. Don't hit a wall because you were looking down or run your e-bike into a car because you weren't paying attention.)

The point is that you get to choose whether or not you make moments. It's about intentionality. There will be times that you miss moments. Just make sure that you're intentional about making moments when it matters.

PART 2

Be the Moment

CHAPTER 5

Get Ready to BREW— Ground Rules for Success

I promised you that this wasn't going to be an all-theory-no-action book. Let's get to the action part with the BREW Method—your psychology-backed framework designed to help you consciously create impactful moments.

What exactly are we brewing? Here's a quick look at the BREW Method:

B: Be the Moment—This is the prep phase, or the way you start making moments *before* you even walk into the room or pick up the phone.

R: Raise Confidence—Power poses, nonverbal communication, how to dress, how to hold your body—this step is about commanding the room (or the Zoom call) with confidence and credibility.

E: Engage—This is where connection happens. If you're tired of hearing about "active listening" without any practical steps, me too—this is different.

W: What About ______?—Let's be honest, interactions aren't always smooth. Clients push back. You forget what you were going to say. Technology glitches. Someone you counted on doesn't show up. This final piece is about learning how to embrace the awkwardness and use it to pivot better, listen better, and make moments in unexpected ways.

(In the resources section of this book, you'll find a copy of this outline to refer to whenever you need it.)

Before we start brewing moments, though, let's cover the ground rules.

Ground Rule 1: Become It, Don't Fake It

You've probably heard the phrase "Fake it till you make it," stemming from Amy Cuddy's famous TED Talk on Power Poses.[8] (Sidenote: this is a must-watch). Here's a fun fact: Amy Cuddy herself isn't a fan of that phrase. It was an off-the-cuff remark that just…stuck (talk about a moment that resonated). She never intended it to be a catchphrase that caught on.

When you learn the pieces of the BREW Method and how to put them into play, you're not going to fake it. In fact, authenticity is a key part of making moments. Instead, you're going to *become it*. You're going to change the way you show up and interact. You're going to step

> **YOU'RE NOT FAKING IT UNTIL YOU MAKE IT. YOU'RE PRACTICING IT UNTIL YOU BECOME IT.**

---

8 Amy Cuddy, "Your Body Language May Shape Who You Are." TED Talk, Edinburgh, Scotland, June 2012, 20 min., 45 sec., https://www.ted.com/talks/amy_cuddy_your_body_language_may_shape_who_you_are?language=en.

into a more powerful version of yourself. And you're going to become the moment maker you need to be.

So let's reframe it. You're not faking it until you make it. You're *practicing it until you become it.*

Ground Rule 2: Shift It, Don't Overhaul It

At the same time, you need to remember that becoming a moment maker doesn't mean changing everything you already know. Instead of trying to overhaul everything, focus on the small changes. In the book *Atomic Habits*, James Clear points out that improving by 1% every day leads to a massive improvement over a year.[9] Those small, intentional shifts add up.

As you work through the chapters that break down the BREW Method, keep that 1% shift in mind.

Think of it like a pour-over coffee—those of you who are obsessed with this know that even the slightest tweak changes your brew (or so I've heard…I am not in the pour-over game). The grams of beans. The temperature of the water. How fine or coarse you grind the beans. Every little change impacts the final cup.

You don't need a full overhaul. You need to find the little changes that create big impact. For each step of the BREW Method, ask yourself: What's the ONE small shift you can make *today* or *this week* to brew better moments?

---

9 James Clear, *Atomic Habits: An Easy & Proven Way to Build Good Habits & Break Bad Ones* (Avery, 2018).

Think small. Think manageable. What's the *one* change you can practice consistently? That's where the magic starts.

Ground Rule 3: Be Consistent, Not Perfect

This brings us to consistency. We all know it's key, but ask yourself…do you *really* do this? I know I fall off the consistency wheel every freaking day.

Why do New Year's resolutions famously fail? Because we're focused on the big goal, instead of the day-to-day consistency. Imagine that everyone in your workplace decided to commit to making ten cold calls a week.

Great idea, right? The first week, everybody accomplishes it. People are feeling good about hitting that goal. But by the second week, the calls haven't really paid off, and we're starting to get pulled in different directions. And, let's be honest, cold calling isn't really our favorite part of the job. But you keep going because the group is committed to it.

By the end of the next week, someone sends a text in the group and says, "I'm so sorry, you guys, I only did five cold calls this week, and I forgot I'm out on vacation tomorrow."

What happens? It gives everyone an out. And before long, the commitment fades away. Why? Because you will find an excuse to not be consistent with things that are challenging or new.

Here's the thing to remember: your goal is the *result* of the habit. And that means the *habit* is where you need to put your focus.

You've set a number, or your company set a number for you to hit this year. And the same the year before and the year before that, right? And what are you doing to make it happen? Traditionally, you've focused on the goal—not the day-to-day to get there.

> **FOCUS ON YOUR CONSISTENCY OF CONNECTION.**

Stop focusing on the number goal and start focusing on your consistency of connection. When you finish this book and life gets busy again, the challenge will be to do it one more day. And then one more day after that.

> **ADAPT, ADJUST, KEEP SHOWING UP, AND DO IT MESSY.**

Now, here's the caveat: Consistency is NOT about perfection. Life happens. You'll have off days. I recently went for a run, planning on a certain distance, but time was tight and I wasn't feeling it. Instead of scrapping the run entirely (breaking consistency), I shortened the distance but picked up the pace (adapting). The impact was still there, the habit was maintained, but it looked different that day. Adapt, adjust, keep showing up, and do it messy (that's life).

Ready to Brew?

Those are your ground rules: Become it, don't fake it. Shift it, don't overhaul it. Be consistent, not perfect. Keep these in mind, and let's get ready to brew moments.

CHAPTER 6

Be the "Moment" in Momentum

Time for the "B" in the Brew Method: Be the Moment in Momentum. We've established that moments matter. And at the same time, isolated moments, however impactful, don't close deals or build relationships. What does?

Sales comes down to *momentum.* How do you consistently move someone forward from one interaction to the next?

In other words, how do you BE the moment in momentum? Meaning, how do you build momentum from the moments you create? The simple formula? Momentum = intention + structure.

> **BE THE MOMENT IN MOMENTUM.**

You need to know where you're going with every interaction and have an organized plan for how to get there.

Sounds simple, right? And yet, I'm guessing you haven't been trained on any of this.

We're trained to have an agenda. We're trained to build relationships. We're *not trained* on how to layer moments together to form momentum.

Thinking About Intention Differently

Let's start by talking about your intention. What are you trying to accomplish from an interaction with a client? Closing a deal? Making the sale. No. Remember; that's the result, not your goal. Your intention needs to be smaller and more focused. And most importantly, it needs to be based on the client's needs.

IF IT'S NOT VALUABLE TO THE CLIENT, IT DOESN'T MATTER.

Moment makers aren't focused on pitching. They aren't focused on themselves. They're focused on value for the client.

Now a note on "value." Value is not "Our product is #1," "Our service is the best," or "Our platform is elite." Toss that out. Let's be clear—that's not the value you bring to the meeting. It might be true. However, if it's not *valuable to the client*, it doesn't matter.

Instead, focus on what your client would truly find valuable. And that means researching and getting curious.

Ask yourself:

- *What's the goal of this interaction?*
- *What are the challenges the client is facing?*
- *What outcomes are they hoping for?*

- *How can I listen and learn what truly matters to them in this conversation?*
- *How do I want the client to feel?*
- *What can I learn?*
- *What value am I offering?*

Sometimes it's as simple as asking, "What's your goal for the meeting today?" Other times, it's helping them see solutions to their problems. It's *always* about them and not you.

If you're thinking, "I already do this," I'm going to challenge you; do you ask this question to *respond* or to actually *learn more*? All too often, we do the former. We ask questions to jump to our pitch or product, when we should really be digging even deeper to learn what truly matters to them.

Digging Deeper: The "Why Funnel"

One of the most powerful ways to cut through the surface noise and truly understand what matters to your client, and to sharpen your own intention for the meeting, is to use the "Why Funnel."

Here's how it works. Think about the client's biggest pain points and ask yourself, or even better, ask your client, why they need your solution. Repeatedly ask, "Why?" until you get deeper and deeper to the real core answer.

Consider the following:

Why do they need our product?

Possible answer: "Because the solution they're currently using isn't working well for them."

Okay, *why* isn't their current solution working well?

"Because their turnaround time with it is too slow; they're not getting information or results quickly enough."

And *why* does that slow turnaround time actually matter to their business?

"Because it's causing significant delays in their internal processes when trying to serve *their* own clients."

And *why* is *that* delay a critical problem for them?

"Because they are losing deals and potential revenue."

Ding, ding, ding! *That's* the real pain and the door to your real value. Your client doesn't "need your product." They need to stop losing deals. Your product is the means to solve that problem. This is where you focus your intention.

Is this easy? No. That's why most people don't focus on it. Do the best salespeople do this? Yes. And that's why you need to learn it.

What is Structure in Sales? (Hint: It's Not What You Think It Is)

Intention is half of our formula for momentum. The other half? Structure. I know we've all heard "structure" over and over and over by now. It's drilled into us from our first day in sales.

But what exactly is it? We think of structure as a plan or a series of steps:

- Reach out to X number of prospects a week
- Get a meeting

- Send a calendar invite
- Have an agenda
- Open with intros
- Move right into the pitch
- Thank them and tell them you'll email a follow-up
- Send a follow-up email two weeks after a cold outreach email

These "structures" are guidelines that we can follow. But are they effective? No. In fact, I would say they aren't even really "structure."

To explain why, let's imagine a group of musicians who all show up with the same sheet music.

They have the plan; the music is right in front of them.

The violins know what to play.

The percussion knows when to hit.

The brass has their cues marked.

But what if there's no conductor? What if nobody's leading the performance? Chaos. Each section may be following the steps, but without a way to bring it all together, the plan doesn't produce something beautiful—it's scattered and not cohesive.

The conductor, on the other hand, brings the steps together.

They set the pace.

They cue each section to enter.

They pull back the flutes so the strings can rise.

The music transforms. It's more than notes being played. It's an experience.

That's the difference between a plan and a structure. Real structure goes beyond a series of steps. It's the way every piece comes together with strategy and intention to create something powerful.

Sales works the same way. Having an agenda or a list of to-dos isn't enough. Structure is you being the conductor, not just a player. That means having the *right plan, strategically* thought out to create momentum. The way you prepare. The way you walk into a room. The way you handle introductions. The way you come across in an email. The way you move the conversation forward. Structure is all of these things working together.

And structure doesn't just apply to meetings or any one piece of the sales puzzle. Every single interaction needs structure:

- A voicemail for a cold prospect
- The cadence you use for outreach or follow-up
- Your CTA
- The way you engage at conferences
- Your response when the client balks at your price

EVERYTHING needs structure. There is no "winging it."

When you wing any interaction with a prospective client, you are losing power. You are losing credibility. And you are forgetting that even though the client might be your world when you're focused on them, you are just a small part of *their world.*

That means that *you* need to be the one driving the action. You cannot make them work harder than they need to or expect them to drive your sales process for you.

The number one frustration I hear when I'm training teams is, "What do I do if a client ghosts me?" If that's happened to you (and who hasn't it happened to?), I can just about guarantee it comes down to your structure, or lack thereof, from the very beginning. You didn't have a plan or if you did it was generic, you left the ball in the client's court, or you just plain weren't clear enough.

Structure is about having a plan of action, from prep to close, for every interaction—and intentionally leading that interaction forward every step of the way.

Is Structure REALLY That Important?

Yes. Even if you "know all the right things to say." Even if you've been in sales for decades. Even if you think you can run a meeting in your sleep. Having a plan, putting in the prep, and knowing how to drive the momentum forward matters.

Why? Several reasons.

The first is that structure *provides psychological safety*. Humans need structure. They crave certainty.[10] It's why clutter stresses you out. It's why you want to have a place for your things in your home. It's why you have a generally predictable routine. Structure gives you a safety net.

---

10 Florian M. Artinger et al., "Coping With Uncertainty: The Interaction of Psychological Safety and Authentic Leadership in Their Effects on Defensive Decision Making," *Journal of Business Research* 190 (2025): 115240, https://doi.org/10.1016/j.jbusres.2025.115240.

Have you ever been pulled into an unplanned meeting or put on the spot with a question you didn't expect? How did it feel? Uncomfortable, right? That's because you didn't have the chance to create structure. You're flailing around without a safety net.

Structure also *builds credibility*. When you take charge of a conversation and step in as a leader, it tells the client that they are in good hands. You know what you're doing. You are organized, professional, and able to handle their needs.

What does it tell them if you just "wing it"? That you can't even lead a conversation. That you didn't prepare. That you aren't reliable. Structure tells them they can count on you.

Finally, structure *creates confidence*. When you've prepared and put a plan in place, you remove unknowns and uncertainty. And when you do that, you can stand stronger in your power. (We'll talk more about confidence in chapter 7).

And what if you are already experienced? Already confident? Know how to do it all? You *still need structure*. Your job is evolving, whether you realize it or not. Sales changes over time. And strategically planning out your structure in place is how you adjust and evolve with it.

Plan to Be Different

One of the best things you can pre-plan is how to *be different*. Different interrupts patterns. Different gets noticed. Different creates an impact. We all know we want to

> **DIFFERENT INTERRUPTS PATTERNS. DIFFERENT GETS NOTICED. DIFFERENT CREATES AN IMPACT.**

stand out. And how exactly do we do that? Not by winging it. Not by hoping you're memorable. By intentionally doing something different. One of my clients, for example, started putting the restaurant menu in the calendar invite when scheduling a lunch or dinner meeting. In the invite, they'd add a note that said, "Looking forward to our lunch. The menu is attached in case you want to take a peek. I'm already eyeing the chicken piccata!" The result? When they arrived for one of these meetings, the client said, "I have been looking forward to this lunch for weeks! I saw the menu you sent, and I've been so excited."

Pause and think about that. When was the last time you had a *first meeting* with someone where they were genuinely *excited* to see you? That rarely happens! The small structural change, adding the menu, broke up the pattern of monotony in the client's inbox, created an anticipation, and fostered a personal touch. It turned the calendar invite into an *experience*.

Think about how you can do *your* calendar invites differently. Find a way to let your personality shine through and word things just differently enough, thoughtfully enough, to break through the inbox monotony and create a moment that builds momentum.

It doesn't have to include a menu. It can be something as simple as, "Looking forward to our conversation. Here are a few topics I'm planning to explore…I'd love to hear what's most top of mind for you so we can shape this together."

Or "Can't wait to dive in. Here are some key topics I would like to focus on…I'd love to hear what's on your radar at the moment."

(Pro tip: Never go over three bullet points when doing this. The human brain can only process so much information at once, and the last thing you want to do is have your client tune out before you've even started connecting.)

The calendar invite is only one example. You can structure something *different* in email subject lines, voicemails, follow-ups, or introductions in meetings. (In part 3, we'll break down how to specifically apply this to each phase of the sales process.)

Plan Your Connection Points

Structure doesn't mean sticking to a script for an entire meeting or forgetting to actually engage with the people in front of you. It *does mean* that you need to plan your connection points.

This comes down to your talk track: the core messages, talking points, relevant stories, and clarifying questions you plan to weave into a conversation.

For example, before a meeting, you can ask yourself:

- What are one to three points that *must* land for this conversation to be successful *for the client*?
- What story can I share that these clients will connect to?
- What questions can I ask to help me get insight into this client?

Jot these down to have on hand to weave into a conversation.

Pro tip: If it sounds like what everyone else is saying, or what you've been saying the same way for over a year, CHANGE IT UP. The same goes for your responses. If they're starting to sound the same, it's time to shift your approach.

Case in point…"any questions?" This is the universal, lazy end to a presentation or explanation. It puts all the onus on the client and rarely yields anything useful. At this point, your client has heard "any questions" so often that they're basically tuning out when you say it.

Try this instead: "Okay, Jamie, we covered quite a bit [recap topic briefly]. What are your initial thoughts or feelings on this specific piece?" It's the same intent, but far more direct, personal, and likely to spark real dialogue. The goal is to stand out and make an impact in the moment.

Plan to Offer Value

You also need to know how to offer value to the client. Plan how you're going to communicate that in a way that puts the focus on what's important to them, *not you*.

Brew It Better	
Instead of this…	Try this…
"Based on what you've told me, our platform would be a great fit. It's built on a new cloud architecture that processes data up to 50% faster than legacy systems like the one you're using. We also offer a fully integrated dashboard that provides real-time analytics on your team's performance."	"It sounds like the core issue we need to solve here is the risk of losing deals simply because your team is stuck waiting for information. This is where I think we can really help. With this platform, your team will be able to get those critical client-facing documents generated in seconds, not hours. This means you can respond to your prospects faster, get ahead of the competition, and ultimately, secure those deals you've been at risk of losing."

Which feels more personal? Which would make *you* want to move forward? The first example sells a feature (speed). The second one sells an outcome (not losing deals). The reframed version speaks directly to the "ding, ding, ding" pain point you uncovered in your "why funnel." It's framed entirely around them, their team, and their results.

Plan, Prep, and Practice

Having the right plan in place matters. So does preparing and practicing. Don't skip out on the pre-work.

Research your client. Know what's important to them. And if you *don't know*, have a plan for the questions you are going to ask to learn what does matter to them. Have notes in front of you to remind you of what you planned to say (these are just prompts; do NOT read them off the paper). And PRACTICE— OUT LOUD.

Practice what you're going to say on a voicemail before you place a call. Practice how you're going to introduce yourself at a networking event. Practice how to close your meeting confidently and clearly. Yes, even if it feels silly. Nobody ever regrets prepping and practicing, but plenty of people regret showing up unprepared.

Build Momentum

When you focus on the two big pieces from this chapter, intention and structure, it paves the way for momentum. Your clients feel more respected and less pushed. They see your credibility and confidence. They know that they are in trusted hands.

If you only did this step (carving out your intention deliberately and creating a structured plan), you would already be moving toward better connection and better sales.

Stop leaning on old habits. Stop thinking your agenda is your structure. Stop defaulting to what feels comfortable if it's not getting you results.

Now, will this new approach work 100% of the time? Of course not. Nothing in sales (or life) does. But I guarantee it will get you way further than the old, passive methods.

Momentum doesn't just happen. You create it. So BE the moment. And let that moment move things forward.

Espresso Shot: *Your Challenge*

Before your very next client interaction (even an email), pause and ask: "What does this client need to get out of this for it to be valuable to them?" Write that answer down as your primary intention above your own goals.

CHAPTER 7

Raise Confidence

B e the moment in momentum? Check. Now, we're on to the R: Raising Confidence.

You might be thinking, "I'm already confident, so I don't need this." Let me call bullshit on that right now. Even the most outwardly confident person in the world practices raising their confidence, consciously or unconsciously.

Confidence is *not* a fixed trait you're either born with or not. It's a learned skill. And if we're going to learn it and practice it, first we need to talk about what it really means.

Here's what confidence is *not*:

- Swagger
- Arrogance
- Being the loudest person in the room

We've all seen insecurity masquerading as confidence. I like to call it "puffer fish" mode. Think of someone who puffs up and comes across as overly confident. They might lean back with their elbows behind their head, forming wing arms, and ask questions they already know the answers to. (I *know* you know someone like this). Guess what? That's not confidence. It's a learned behavior—a defense mechanism for feeling uncomfortable, insecure, or out of control.

Flipping the Narrative: Confidence the BREW Way

So…what does "real" confidence look like? There's not necessarily one right answer. Daniel Pink once wrote that "true confidence isn't about unwavering certainty—it's about balancing conviction with curiosity. Confidence builds trust; curiosity fosters growth."[11] In other words, confidence means more than being "sure of yourself." It means both believing in yourself and being open to asking questions, growing, and learning.

Some people exude confidence because they are deeply knowledgeable and passionate about their subject. Others are confident precisely because they own their awkwardness with humor and authenticity, making them incredibly relatable. Some people show confidence by leaning into learning and staying curious. There are multiple ways to be confident.

Let's take a look at two people who exuded confidence in very distinct and different ways: Jane Goodall and Cary Grant.

Jane Goodall (a zoologist and anthropologist known for her work with chimpanzees) entered the workforce at a time when

---

11 Daniel Pink, "True confidence isn't about unwavering certainty. It's about balancing conviction with humility," Facebook, December 19, 2024, https://www.facebook.com/danielhpink/posts/true-confidence-isnt-about-unwavering-certainty-its-about-balancing-conviction-w/1112782173558856/.

women were often not working outside of the home, let alone becoming scientists. But she didn't let that shake her. She focused on her passion, her authentic self, and her goal to work with animals. She exuded a quiet confidence, which allowed her to observe and notice things that other people didn't. This led to discoveries about chimpanzees and their behavior that had never before been revealed, particularly around how much their behavior is similar to human behavior. Her confidence, which was intentional and focused instead of loud and commanding, changed science and our understanding of primates.

On the other end of the spectrum is Cary Grant, an actor in the 1940s known for his commanding presence. He grew up dirt poor and had a rough childhood. When he started acting, he observed the people around him that he was drawn to and eventually adopted those traits to then incorporate in the roles he was cast in. He later said, "I pretended to be somebody I wanted to be until finally I became that person. Or the persona became me. Or we met at some point."[12] He developed a persona that worked for him, a much louder, more noticeable confidence than Jane Goodall's.

So…which kind of confidence is "real"? The quiet, focused confidence of Jane Goodall? Or the more commanding swagger of Cary Grant? Both. Why? They were both authentic. They were both curious. And they both stood firm in who they were while also learning from the world around them. Jane's quiet confidence let her feel powerful, able to shut out the outside world that told her what she should and shouldn't be.

---

12 Marc Eliot, *Cary Grant: A Biography* (Crown, 2004).

And Cary's confidence let him feel powerful, able to show up and express his art in a way that reflected his personality.

That's what confidence really is in the BREW Method: authentic ways to feel powerful and grounded in who you are.

When you show up with authentic confidence, it draws people to you and makes them want to be a part of your orbit. That's why confidence is emphasized so often in sales. So where are so many salespeople going wrong?

We're focusing too much on how to show or prove our confidence and not enough on the psychology of what actually *makes us more confident to begin with.*

If we can reframe it and learn to create our own authentic confidence, communicating and exuding confidence becomes easy. (No "faking it" necessary, remember?) That's where we're going to start: learning how to raise our own confidence. From there, we'll cover how to project it in every room, Zoom, or whatever setting we find ourselves in.

Confidence Part 1: Own It

Have you ever walked into a meeting room where the energy just felt flat? Or maybe thick with tension? What's your usual move? If you're like most people, you probably adjust your own energy down to match, maybe try to blend in.

For moment makers, there's a change: *You don't shift your energy for the room; you shift the room's energy to yours.*

YOU DON'T SHIFT YOUR ENERGY FOR THE ROOM; YOU SHIFT THE ROOM'S ENERGY TO YOURS.

And that means stepping up as a leader and owning your presence and power. In any group setting, people subconsciously scan the room, searching for cues of confidence and leadership. Think about the last conference or networking event you attended. Who were you drawn to? My guess is it was the people who seemed grounded, open, engaged, and comfortable in their own skin.

That doesn't always come easily though. If you find yourself feeling nervous or uncomfortable in group settings or when speaking in a meeting, you're not alone.

How do you ground yourself and boost your confidence? One way is to remember *who you are*. I don't care if you don't have the most prestigious title. I don't care if you're new or inexperienced or young. (How many times have you seen someone who's been in sales for years that knows nothing? Or someone who has a title they really didn't earn? It happens all the time.)

Know your worth. Know your value. *You* are in the room *for a reason.*

Confidence Part 2: Embody It

You saw the power of body language in action in the stories about Starbucks Kid, Elevator CEO, and Gym Lady. This matters more than you realize. Why?

Your body language isn't just about communicating with others. It's also about communicating with yourself. The way you hold your body impacts your mood and your emotions— your body tells your brain how to feel.

When it comes to how you hold your body, think big versus little, open versus closed. Big, but not exaggerated postures (shoulders back, chest open, taking up space) don't just look more confident; they actually make you feel more confident.

Amy Cuddy's work on Power Poses brought this idea to mainstream attention. Putting your hands on your hips or out wide to your side? Standing with your chest out and your feet apart? These things create confidence. If you're a *Ted Lasso* fan, remember the way Rebecca eased her anxiety by making her whole body bigger, layered with the younger version of herself? It was a powerful moment that showed the impact your body can have on your brain.

Your posture *portrays* confidence and *creates confidence*. There's plenty of evidence to back this up. Research shows that adopting powerful, open postures actually increases feelings of confidence and lowers stress hormones like cortisol.[13] It's a biochemical reality.

In one study, researchers observed hundreds of athletes from more than 30 different countries around the world, some of whom were blind from birth. When the athletes won they instinctively adopted winning poses: arms raised, chest out, head tilted up—even those who were blind and had never seen someone do so. When they lost, they slumped into low-power poses: shoulders hunched, head down.[14] These are innate

---

13 Robert Korner et al., "Dominance and prestige: Meta-analytic review of experimentally induced body position effects on behavioral, self-report, and physiological dependent variables," *Psychological Bulletin* 148, no. 1-2 (2022): 67-85, https://doi.org/10.1037/bul0000356.

14 Ed Yong, "Blind Olympic Athletes Show the Universal Nature of Pride and Shame," *National Geographic*, August 13, 2008, https://www.nationalgeographic.com/science/article/blind-olympic-athletes-show-the-universal-nature-of-pride-and-shame.

expressions of dominance and submission, hardwired into our biology.

Your posture can also send a lot of other signals. It can invite others in or tell them you're closed off to their ideas. It can create a relaxed, warm atmosphere or communicate fear or tension. The way you hold your shoulders, the way you position your arms and legs, how stiff your body is, whether you're sitting up straight or slouched over…it's all part of communication.

Imagine you were on a date, sitting across from someone at dinner, and they had their arms crossed and were leaning as far back as they could. Or that they were slouched forward, hunched over their menu the entire time. What would that feel like? Would they seem interested, engaged, and receptive? No.

Arms at your sides can signal openness. Leaning forward shows that you're interested and engaged. Leaning back or angling your shoulders away from someone signals that you are ready to leave or uninterested in what they have to say. Holding your shoulders tensely and tightly shows that you're feeling strained or stressed. Relaxing your shoulders shows that you're calm and receptive.

To really see this in action, spend some time in front of a mirror and try out these body positions:

- Stand with your legs together and cross your arms, holding your shoulders tensely.
- Separate your feet and spread your arms wide.
- Pull up a chair and put your hands behind your head, leaning back.

- Put your hands at your side and let your shoulders drop.
- Lean forward with your hands in your lap.

How did each of these positions *look*? How did they feel? What did you notice about yourself? Each position sent different signals, right? This is why it's so important to be aware of your body, especially if you're feeling nervous, tense, or unsure of yourself. It just takes a small adjustment to make a difference.

To communicate confidence, openness, and receptivity, aim for the following:

- Relaxed shoulders and arms
- "Fronting," or pointing your body at the person speaking or the person you're speaking to
- Arms and legs uncrossed
- Back straight, but not too stiff

This is how you raise your confidence and send it into the world. Presence is power. Presence is possibility.

Confidence Part 3: Exude It

Your posture isn't the only way to project confidence. The 7-38-55 rule is a psychological model that describes how people communicate emotions through words, tone of voice, and body language. According to the rule, just 7% of our communication happens with words, 55% comes from body language and facial expressions, and 38% from "ornaments" (how you appear, including your clothing and style).[15]

---

15 Albert Mehrabian and Susan R. Ferris, "Inference of Attitudes From Nonverbal Communication in Two Channels," *Journal of Consulting Psychology* 31, no. 3 (1967): 248–252, https://doi.org/10.1037/h0024648.

Add that up, and a whopping 93% of the initial impression you make, the confidence you project, and the trust you build happens apart from the words you say.

(Important to note: the actual number has been questioned and hasn't been confirmed outside of the two original studies that promoted this concept. The general consensus is that the number itself might not be measurable, but that the overall takeaway is accurate. Most communication happens nonverbally.)

Let's break down the other elements involved in exuding confidence:

Hands

Believe it or not, hands are one of the first things people notice, even if it's subconscious. Why? It's primal. Back in caveman days, seeing someone's hands told you if they were holding a weapon (foe) or were open and perhaps offering food (friend). That instinct is still wired into us. We subconsciously look at hands to gauge safety and trustworthiness. They are major trust factors.

And it isn't just where our hands are positioned that matters; it's also what they're doing. One study analyzed viral TED Talks, trying to determine why some took off when the content quality was generally high across the board. The results showed that speakers in the most popular talks used significantly more hand gestures.[16] Hand gestures signal passion, openness, and confidence, which resonates deeply with audiences.

Hands are a big visual cue. In fact, if someone holds up three fingers but says the number five, people are more likely to remember the number as *three*, despite what you said. The visual impact is stronger.

We want our hands open and visible. We want to use purposeful gestures. And we definitely don't want to be fidgeting, rubbing our hands together, holding a phone, or playing with our hair.

The problem is that many of us don't even *think* about what we're doing with our hands. In fact, when you first start thinking about it, it's probably going to feel awkward. Don't worry, you're not the only one who suddenly thinks, "Um, what do I usually do with my hands? Why do they feel like they're in the way?" You won't always feel clunky. (Practice it until you become it).

If you struggle with hand positioning at first, help yourself out along the way. Can't seem to help moving your hands around? Use a stabilizer, like a pen or a coffee cup. Don't fidget with it. Use it to keep your hands grounded. Can't stop playing with your hair or jewelry? Pull your hair up and minimize jewelry. Tend to adjust your tie? Hold a pen to keep your hands occupied. Using a coffee cup as a stabilizer and pulling my hair up are my personal go-tos. The coffee cup keeps my hands in view without me having to think about it and having my hair pulled back removes the possibility of messing with it. Do

---

16 Alison Prato, "Does Body Language Help a TED Talk Go Viral? 5 Nonverbal Patterns From Blockbuster Talks," *TED Blog*, May 12, 2015, https://blog.ted.com/body-language-survey-points-to-5-nonverbal-features-that-make-ted-talks-take-off/.

what it takes to make yourself comfortable while you build new habits with the way you use your hands.

Brew It Better	
Don't...	Do...
<ul><li>Hide your hands in your pockets. This reads as deceptive or insecure.</li><li>Engage in anxious movements or self-soothing gestures: cracking knuckles, fiddling with jewelry, or touching your face or hair.</li><li>Let your phone become a blocker. Holding it creates a physical barrier and often pulls you into a low-power posture. Put it away.</li></ul>	<ul><li>Keep your hands visible. Your hands should always be out of your pockets, resting naturally where they can be seen. If it feels comfortable, place them on the table. If that doesn't feel right, put your hands in your lap and make sure that your chair is pulled back enough so that they can still be seen.</li><li>Use a stabilizer, such as a pen or a coffee cup, to keep your hands occupied. Just don't fidget with the object.</li><li>Think about your palm placement; open palms convey trust.</li><li>Use natural gestures that match your words.</li><li>On virtual calls: Ensure your camera framing is waist-up so gestures are visible. When listening, try the "computer face," resting your chin lightly on your hand (still visible!) and leaning in to show interest.</li></ul>

Eyes

Eye contact is the most obvious nonverbal cue, but are you really nailing it? Genuine eye contact does something amazing chemically: it helps release oxytocin, the bonding hormone. It's the neurochemical equivalent of a good hug from a trusted friend. So, in a business setting, it builds rapport, connection, and credibility instantly.

Focus on maintaining eye contact. Easy enough, right? Especially if you're meeting just one or two people in person. It feels more complicated in a remote setting or when you're meeting a larger group.

For example in a virtual meeting, you might think you're making eye contact when you look at the other person's face on your screen, but to them, you're looking down or away. Instead, practice looking directly into the camera lens. This is almost definitely going to feel wrong at first, but it will feel right to the person you're speaking to. If you have trouble remembering, put a sticky note at the top of your computer to remind you. And, if you use dual screens, be extra mindful of where your gaze is falling. It's helpful to record yourself and play it back so you can see exactly what other people actually experience.

What about group settings? With more than three to five people, the tendency is to scan vaguely over everyone's heads. Instead, remember the "rule of three." Intentionally select three individuals in different parts of the room and rotate between them, making genuine, brief eye contact with each as you speak.

Phew. That's a lot to think about just for posture, hands, and eyes, right? Master them, and you're well on your way to projecting confidence that lets you create powerful moments. Remember to focus on your *own* nonverbal cues; don't overanalyze or make assumptions about other people's. In his book, *What Every Body is Saying,* Joe Navarro establishes "ten commandments" for reading non-verbal cues. One of those is to pay attention to pattern shifts when observing people's body language.[17] Everyone has a baseline, and you don't know what anyone else's is. For example, one person might cross their arms when they're closed off, but another person might fall into it as a baseline stance. Maybe they're just cold. Maybe they're used to doing it that way. You can't know. Instead, look for pattern shifts. Were they open and now closed off? Did they lean forward suddenly? Pattern shifts can give us insight into what's going on for other people.

Ornaments: Dress, Brand, and Color

I would love to tell you that nothing about your appearance matters. The truth is that it *does.* Your clothing, your grooming, your accessories: it's how you visually package yourself and show competence, confidence, and credibility. And, just like with posture, the effect goes both ways—how you dress also impacts how you feel and perform.

Dressing for Power

Let's start with the basics. Well-fitted, professional attire signals competence and attention to detail. Notice I didn't say

---

17 Joe Navarro and Marvin Karlins, *What Every Body Is Saying: An Ex-FBI Agent's Guide to Speed-Reading People* (New York: HarperCollins, 2008), 45.

expensive. A well-fitting, clean outfit from Target beats an ill-fitting, sloppy designer suit any day. Fit and condition are key.

Does it really matter? Yes. Why? Because of something called "enclothed cognition." This is a psychological phenomenon that shows that our clothing influences our emotions, attitude, and performance.

One notable example of enclothed cognition came from a study that conducted academic tests on participants. The first time, they wore their regular clothing, and the second time they were given white lab coats to wear over that same clothing. The results showed that people scored higher on tests when wearing the lab coats. And to drive it home, the study included another experiment. This time, two groups of participants were given the same coat to wear—but one group was told it was a medical doctor's coat while the other was told it was a painter's coat. The group that believed they were wearing medical doctors' coats scored significantly higher.[18]

Other studies have shown that dressing more formally increases your feelings of power and leads to enhanced abstract thinking.[19] In a study on negotiations, participants secured more profitable deals when dressed in suits than in sweatpants.

---

18 Hajo Adam and Adam D. Galinsky, "Enclothed Cognition," *Journal of Experimental Social Psychology* 48, no. 4 (2012): 918–925, https://www.sciencedirect.com/science/article/abs/pii/S0022103112000200.

19 Michael L. Slepian et al., "The Cognitive Consequences of Formal Clothing," *Social Psychological and Personality Science* 6, no. 6 (2015): 661–68, https://doi.org/10.1177/1948550615579462.

In other words, dressing like a leader makes you *feel* and *act* more like a leader.[20]

This is often called "The Blazer Effect." Simply putting on a more structured piece of clothing like a blazer can make you physically sit taller, adjust your posture, speak more deliberately, and feel more powerful and capable. It literally changes your presence from the outside in. (And yes, that effect still kicks in even if you're rocking pajama bottoms below the frame on a Zoom call!)

Knowing Your Audience (and Your Authentic Style)

Okay, so dressing professionally makes a difference. And what does that look like in the real world? It's rarely one-size-fits-all. This is where you navigate the balancing act between industry norms, your audience, and your own authentic self.

Pay attention to the visual norms in your industry. Finance tends to be more conservative and formal than, say, a creative agency. Some workplaces are jeans and a blazer settings. Some have a tennis shoe culture. If you work at Google, showing up in a suit would be weird; everyone in the room is going to be dressed casually.

Also, consider your audience for a specific interaction. Meeting the C-suite likely calls for a different level of formality than a casual check-in with someone in your network.

---

20 Michael W. Kraus and Wendy Berry Mendes, "Sartorial Symbols of Social Class Elicit Class-Consistent Behavioral and Physiological Responses: A Dyadic Approach," *Journal of Experimental Psychology: General* 143, no. 6 (2014): 2330-40, https://doi.org/10.1037/xge0000023.

Know your setting, and know your audience. For example, I have a long-term client who I know well. When I conduct in-person trainings for his team, I wear a blazer, dress pants, and heels—prime stereotypical professional dress. And I also know that when I meet that client virtually, he's in an old t-shirt. So when I have Zoom meetings with him, I'm a lot more laid back. I can just toss on a sweater and have my hair pulled up in a bun.

It's also important to stay authentic to your personal style. That doesn't mean you can roll into a conference in sweatpants and a hoodie just because that's what you prefer on your down-time; you can build your personality into professional dress. This can mean adding a personal "power piece" to a professional outfit. For men, this might mean patterned socks, adding a pop of color to a suit. Or a unique tie or pocket square. For women, this could be a statement necklace or bright heels. A go-to for me is big hoop earrings and bold, colorful heels with otherwise neutral outfits. It became part of my signature—professional, but undeniably me.

I recently heard a group of young men talking about someone who was wearing "Deal Sleds." That caught my attention right away. I asked them what it was, and they told me, "Oh, you know, Gucci shoes that guys in sales wear." I pictured exactly what they were talking about—high-end loafers I've seen on many pairs of feet in the corporate world. Maybe you need your "Deal Sleds" to feel powerful.

One of my clients was prepping for a headquarters meeting at his company. He intentionally wore fun patterned socks to give himself confidence and serve as a conversation starter.

Think about what makes *you* feel confident. I know a woman in her 60s who has been in business for decades. She feels most confident in a skirt—wearing pants doesn't give her the same effect it might give someone fresh out of college.

I remember once when I was dating my now-husband. He picked me up to go out for dinner, and he was wearing a textured suit with a pattern that I thought was over-the-top. I remember thinking. "Hmm, not sure about *that* outfit." And yet, over dinner, probably half a dozen people that walked by complimented him. Could everyone pull that off? Definitely not. He was true to his authentic style. He wore it with confidence. And that approach worked, despite my initial opinion.

The goal is to be yourself while sticking to well-fitted attire, catered to the setting you're in.

Being well-dressed and put together makes people see you as more organized, successful, and trustworthy. On the other hand, if you see someone in public looking disheveled, you often make judgments (fair or not). Appearance sends loud signals.

As a disclaimer, it's important to remember that norms around dress are heavily influenced by culture, region, identity, and environment. What reads as powerful and appropriate here in the US business world might be different elsewhere. Always observe and adapt with awareness. While your use case might be different, be intentional about the way you dress, your physical presence, and how you present yourself.

Incorporating Color Psychology

Beyond fit and style, the colors you choose send potent subconscious messages. Here are some common associations:

- Navy: Trust, stability, dependability—a go-to for finance or leadership
- Black: Authority, sophistication, power—can be very strong
- Gray: Neutrality, balance, logic—incredibly versatile
- White: Cleanliness, organization, detail-orientation—classic crispness
- Bolds (Red, green, etc.): Confidence, energy, attention-grabbing—use strategically

Remember that how colors and styles are perceived isn't always straightforward, especially when gender enters the mix. Welcome to social construct.

Red on anyone can convey confidence, but it might sometimes be perceived as "too aggressive" or "provocative" on women. Gray signals maturity on men, but can sometimes make women seem less impactful if they're trying to build a strong personal brand. Black reads as high status on men but can sometimes feel "too severe" on women if not balanced with lighter colors. Navy, on the other hand, is often seen as a "safe" power color for women, authoritative yet approachable.

Knowing this, I often choose strategically. If I'm walking into a room I know will be all men, I might wear black to project clear authority. If it's a mixed group, I often opt for navy to ensure approachability isn't sacrificed. If I know the team well? Game on for whatever feels right that day. The key is being intentional based on your goal and audience.

Using Pops of Color Strategically

Our eyes go to color first, especially in a sea of neutrals. Regardless of your base outfit, any strategic pop of bright color will get you noticed and add personality. This is fantastic for making an impression on virtual calls or in large rooms. Think: a vibrant tie or scarf, bold lipstick or nail polish, or colorful shoes. If head-to-toe color isn't your thing (it's often not mine), a pop is an easy way to stand out authentically.

Putting It All Together: Confidence is Muscle Memory

At the beginning of this chapter, I called bullshit on anyone saying to themselves, "I'm already confident." Now do you see why? Confidence isn't something you have or don't have. It's something you *create* intentionally. This chapter has the pieces of the puzzle, but you still need to put them all together. And once you do, it becomes habit.

The more you pay attention to your body language, the easier it becomes to fall into powerful postures and use your hands and eyes to create trust. The more you dress for success, the more comfortable you become. You're not just acting confident; you're wiring yourself to be confident by practicing it until you become it.

And when you commit to creating confidence and you nail it, something magical happens. The people around you feel more at ease. They see your confidence and it gives *them* confidence.

Think about any time you've sat in a group and heard a speaker ask for volunteers. What usually happens? Crickets, at first. However, when one person steps up and raises their hand or goes to the front of the room, their confidence becomes contagious. It gives other people permission to be *themselves*.

That's what you're doing when you embody confidence. You're commanding the room and creating an environment where people can both trust you to lead them and feel confident in their own skin. And *that* is a memorable experience.

Espresso Shot: Your Challenge

Power pose: Before your next meeting, stand in a "power pose" (open stance, arms wide, feet wide) for two minutes. Notice how it impacts your confidence walking into a room (or hopping on a virtual call).

CHAPTER 8

Engage

Time to move on to E: Engage. And just like with the B and the R, we're going to start with what engagement doesn't mean.

Usually when we hear "engagement" in sales, what are we talking about? Face time, face time, face time, right? Getting in front of as many clients as possible as many times as we can (or showing up at networking events and being seen at conferences).

When we think about engagement this way, we tend to just throw money at it with schmoozing or gifts or events. And if that works for you, more power to you. But it's not engagement.

Truth time: Clients don't want to be schmoozed. They want value, connection, and trust. Face time doesn't guarantee that.

It's like spending quality time with a partner. You can be in the same room with each other without engaging. You can even be having a conversation about the weather or taxes or chores. It's face time, right? But is it quality time? Is it engagement?

Is it anything worth basing a deep relationship on? Nope. Schmoozing is the same. Simply spending more time with clients isn't enough. And it is a waste of everyone's time.

Think back to the story I shared at the beginning of the book, where I was building a great relationship but missed out on building credibility. Spending time with clients isn't enough. You need to make sure that the time you do spend with clients leads to value, connection, and trust.

Flipping the Narrative:

The answer is not MORE face time; it's BETTER face time. Engagement the BREW way means crafting and cultivating genuine conversations and connections.

Here's the frustrating part: a lot of you have figured out that the hustle and surface-level connections aren't working. You know that you *should* listen more intently, ask better questions, and focus on the client, not just your pitch.

Why is it so hard to do that consistently? Simple. We fall back into familiar patterns. Why? Because autopilot feels safe. Patterns feel predictable. There's comfort in what we know. Sticking to the script we've rehearsed or asking the same questions we always ask gives us a false sense of control.

It's the same instinct that might make us beeline for the bar the second we walk into an awkward networking event: Grab that drink first to create a little buffer before actually having to talk to strangers. It's why we fill an awkward silence in conversation with predictable chatter about the weather instead of daring to ask a more meaningful question. These are our conversational safety nets, the comfortable defaults we grab onto when genuine engagement feels too risky, requires too much vulnerability, or just feels like too much damn effort.

Sound familiar? We all have them. And those safety nets are exactly where meaningful connection goes to die. They keep interactions superficial. They prevent you from being truly present and spotting those subtle cues and opportunities to connect at a deeper level.

They are moment killers.

To create real engagement, you have to consciously interrupt your patterns. You need to catch yourself reaching for the easy, comfortable default behavior and deliberately choose a different one, even if it feels a little awkward at first. And the best place to start is with the most fundamental pattern interrupter of all: curiosity.

> **YOU HAVE TO CONSCIOUSLY INTERRUPT YOUR PATTERNS.**

Stay Curious

Forget your pitch, forget your agenda, forget sounding smart. The single most powerful driver of meaningful engagement is *curiosity*. The best engagers aren't focused on talking about themselves or their solutions; they are genuinely curious about *the other person*. Before your next meeting, call, or even important email, consciously shift into curiosity mode. Does that sound hard? That's because it IS. We're talking about undoing lifelong patterns. The good news is, you can start one small step at a time. This sounds ridiculously simple, maybe even pointless, but trust me on this one. Get your notebook or meeting agenda. At the very top, in big letters, write: STAY CURIOUS.

> **THE SINGLE MOST POWERFUL DRIVER OF MEANINGFUL ENGAGEMENT IS CURIOSITY.**

It might sound cheesy, but let me tell you a little story. I found a recipe on the internet for an amazing spring pasta recipe. It's light, lemony, salty, with asparagus, capers...and raisins. Raisins! The first time I saw that, I thought, "No way." But right after listing raisins, the recipe note said, "(Just do it. You'll thank me later.)" And you know what? Those unexpected raisins absolutely *make* the entire dish.

Now I'm going to give you the same advice about writing "STAY CURIOUS" at the top of the page. It's a visual nudge to interrupt your default patterns. Just do it, you'll thank me later.

Don't Forget the Visual

Engagement actually begins with visuals; psychologically, we connect visually first, before spoken word.

An interesting study conducted on radiologists highlighted this: radiologists were given scans to analyze. When those scans included *patient photos*, the diagnoses were more accurate. In fact, three months later, they were shown the same scans without photos. Their interpretations were less accurate the second time.[21] The visual connection created a better outcome and better performance for the radiologists.

---

21 sYehonatan Turner and Irith Hadas-Halpern, "The Effects of Including a Patient's Photograph to the Radiographic Examination," *Radiological Society of North America, Chicago, IL* (2008)

How do you embrace that reality? Don't neglect your visuals. Put your photograph in your email signature; it's a strong way to start engaging with prospective clients before you even meet them.

Chatting on the phone? Take a minute to pull up the LinkedIn photo of the person you're speaking to—visual connection goes both ways. Looking at the picture will help you build stronger engagement from your side, which leads to more connection and engagement on their end.

And on your own end, make sure your LinkedIn profile picture is up-to-date and professional; people will be looking at it and forming opinions before they even see you.

These are 1% shifts that can make a big difference, and they're just the tip of the iceberg when it comes to engagement.

Learn How to REALLY Listen

I know you've heard the term active listening so many times that it has lost its meaning. So once again, let's dig past the buzzword and talk about what it actually means.

The truth is that we're not actually taught how to listen. We're taught from an early age to *be quiet*, but that's not the same thing.

Have you ever been in an argument with a partner or a friend, and they said something that you disagreed with? What happens? Even if you know you should wait and let them finish saying their side, you're already forming your response in your mind, right? It takes a lot of self-awareness and practice (and sometimes couples therapy) to break this pattern.

The same thing happens in workplace conversations, especially in sales. We're not listening to *hear the other person*. We're listening to *respond*. Our minds are jumping ahead to the next thing we're going to say instead of focusing on truly listening to what the other person is saying.

Imagine that you called a friend to vent about your day, and the conversation went like this:

"Ugh I had the worst day ever! It started with spilling my coffee this morning and went downhill from there."

"Oh that's the worst! Last week I was getting in the car and did the same thing. My car still smells like coffee."

Yikes. They didn't listen to you or your needs *at all*. They jumped right into talking about themselves.

In sales, we do this all the time. It sounds something like this:

You: "And how long have you been with X company?"

Them: "Oh about three years."

You: "Okay, great, let me tell you about how we do XYZ…."

When we do this, we're missing the moment in front of us to jump into whatever it is we want them to know about our product or service.

How much more impactful would it be to stop and engage with what they are saying?

Brew It Better	
Instead of this…	Try this…
You: "And how long have you been with X company?" Them: "Oh about three years." You: "Okay, great, let me tell you about how we do XYZ…."	You: "And how long have you been with X company?" Them: "Oh about three years." You: "And what do you like about them?" Or.. "And how is that working for you?"

Which of these shows that you value the other person's time, thoughts, and needs? And which of these is going to give you more information to help form connections?

Think about the last time you had to call a generic customer service line. You can *hear* the script coming from the other end of the phone. It doesn't matter what you say—the response is going to be the same. And it feels like you're not even talking to a human being. They're only focused on their response, not on listening to you.

If you're listening to respond, you're almost guaranteed to miss moments. After all, moments happen from being present, being curious, and paying attention to what's right in front of you. You can't do that if you're in your head, thinking about the next question or the next part of your pitch you want to get to.

What do you do instead? You start by flipping the switch from "listening to respond" to "listening to hear."

As Simon Sinek says, "Listening is more than the act of hearing—it's creating an environment in which the other person FEELS heard."[22]

One of the best tools to begin with is the power of the pause. Practice taking a beat after someone speaks before you respond—before you even *formulate* a response. Let their words land, and pause and reflect on what they just said before you open your mouth to say anything. This interrupts your pattern and gives you the chance to engage and let the other person know you *heard them* (not just the words they said, but the meaning, the needs, and the emotions behind the words).

Then, instead of moving on to talking about yourself, ask a question or try to get them to keep sharing. Respond with, "Tell me more," or use the Why Funnel from chapter 7 to continue exploring and learning about what really matters to them.

Another tool is mirroring; repeat what the other person said back to them in question form to encourage them to elaborate. For example, if they say, "I'm concerned about our turnaround times," you can respond with, "Turnaround times?"

Mirroring works for several reasons:

- It forces you to respond instead of jumping ahead to your next point;
- It immediately shows the other person that they are being heard;

22 Simon Sinek, "The Art of Listening," Facebook, November 19, 2021, 3 min., 2 sec., https://www.facebook.com/simonsinek/videos/the-art-of-listening/588157329070413/

- It keeps the focus on them instead of you and your product; and
- Perhaps most importantly, it opens the door for them to share more information.

Ultimately, the point of listening is to learn as much as you can about the other person and to show them that you care about hearing what they are saying.

Make no mistake; this isn't an easy switch to flip. You're almost programmed to do the opposite. That's what makes such an impact when you *do* truly listen. People notice it. They feel seen and heard. And they want to keep engaging with you.

Stop Asking Questions You Already Know the Answer To

One of the most unintentional poor communication patterns we fall into is asking questions we either already know the answer to or could easily find out.

Let's say you connected with someone on LinkedIn. And yet, when you meet with them, you ask, "So, how long have you been with the company?" even though the answer is right in their profile.

Why do we do this? It's a comfort mechanism. It's the conversational equivalent of making a beeline for the bar at a networking event before talking to anyone. It's a buffer against discomfort.

But what does it signal to the other person? That you haven't done your homework, that you're not really present, and that you're not truly curious. Your credibility takes an instant hit.

What's better? Using the information you have from their profile to ask a better, deeper question. Instead of "How long have you been here?" try "I saw on LinkedIn you've been leading this team for 15 years. That's impressive longevity. Can you tell me a bit about how the industry has shifted from your perspective during that time?"

What does *this* tell the other person? That you're prepared. That you're curious. That you're interested in their thoughts and insights.

Okay, so you're interrupting bad listening habits by asking better questions and truly hearing the answers. Now let's flip the coin and focus on the other half of powerful engagement: speaking with intention and impact.

Speak With Impact

Listening is a big piece of the puzzle, but what about speaking? How you speak and the specific words you choose matters.

When it comes to maximizing the impact of your words, two key areas make a world of difference: *how* you frame your message and the *specific language* you use. Let's tackle framing first.

You-Framing

In the last chapter, I pointed out that thinking about the value to your client sets the stage for better communication. Here's where you put that into action. The old way of pitching is all about "us." We offer XYZ. Our product is the best. I want to show you _____.

Those statements are all focused on you, not on your client.

Instead, you can shift the language slightly with "you-framing," wording your sentences in a way that puts the focus on the other person.

For example, instead of "This software has advanced analytics," try "This software will help you gain a competitive edge with detailed insights into your market." See the difference?

Brew It Better	
Instead of this...	Try this...
I-Framing	You-Framing
"We offer 24/7 customer service support."	"You can reach us 24/7."
"I think ______."	"What are your thoughts on ______?"
"I want to show you ______."	"You'll find ______."
"I'm just following up to see if you're still interested."	"Let's schedule a call to answer any questions you might have."

The tiniest shift in words can put the focus on the right place and personalize your communication for the person you're speaking to.

The Words You Choose Matter

You-framing isn't the only example of the power of word choice. Your words can either diminish your credibility or create impact. When you choose words that weaken your message or your authority, you take away your own credibility.

For example, I once worked with a team who kept saying, "we're small but mighty." What they didn't realize is that little "but" was indicating that there was something wrong with being a small team, that they had to make up for their size. This phrase unintentionally minimized the power their team had. I called them on it: "Are you small *but* mighty? Or are you small *and* mighty?" The "and" made all the difference.

"But" negates and detracts. "And" connects and sells. "But" is a word that diminishes. "And" is a word with impact.

Another common example is "I'm sorry." That phrase minimizes your power. A simple reframe from "I'm sorry I'm late," to "Thank you for your patience," conveys the same message while holding onto your strength.

Here are some words to avoid using:

Words That Diminish
Just
Maybe
Kind of
But
Sorry
Follow up
I think

Consider the following: Instead of "I'm just following up to see if you're still interested," try "Let's schedule a call to answer any questions you might have."

Instead of "I think that we could try approaching this in a different way," try "Let's do this differently."

The words you use frame your mindset and change the way you see yourself and the way you show up. A negotiator I worked with once told me that he felt "kind of fake" for using communication techniques to advance negotiations in his favor. I reframed it: "You're not being fake; you're *influencing to connect.*" Same action, totally different mindset and energy. Language shapes reality.

The Big Picture: Choosing the "Right" Words

There are a lot of practical tips here that can help you improve your communication. And at the same time, I want you to remember that consciously shaping your language goes beyond just avoiding a few words that diminish or remembering to use "you."

The way we communicate matters. Like with body language, words have their own kind of charisma. When we hear somebody speak really well, when their words just hit right and resonate, it can almost feel like magic. And, like with body language or any of the other confidence pieces we talked about, these skills can be learned, and most importantly, adapted to be authentic for *you.*

I have one client in particular who is an absolute master at business jargon in the most impressive, articulate way. He's incredibly eloquent, and every time I talk to him, he levels me up; his way of speaking attracts people and pushes everyone around him to be better.

Now, if you haven't noticed by the way this book is written, that polished, highly formal style is pretty much the opposite of my natural communication. I can envy his skill sometimes. I can also choose to embody it…in my own way. People generally respond well to the more direct, sometimes edgier, format that I use. It would be weird and inauthentic for me to try and completely overhaul my natural style to mimic his.

Should I use his style of communication for the sake of sounding "better?" No. Should I observe what makes his communication so effective—the precision, the clarity, the confidence—and take a percentage of that to make my communication even better, in my own way? Absolutely.

Next-Level Communication: Connection and Impact

Moving on from the best practices for listening and speaking, there's another element of engagement and communication that matters: connection and impact.

This is where you take the tips and tricks and remember that what matters most is creating a moment that resonates.

The first piece here is to remember that what you *mean* to say isn't always what the other person *hears*. We judge ourselves by our intentions, but others judge us by the *impact* our words and actions have on them.

This happens in our personal lives all the time. I'm the kind of person who has a place for everything; my keys go in the same spot when I walk in the door. My husband, on the other hand, his keys live wherever they are placed on any given day. One day after he came back in the house to find his keys I asked, "So is this something you have always done or is it new?"

My *intention* with my question was curiosity. I feel myself getting more forgetful with age and wondered if it was similar for him. The *impact*? He heard judgment and walked out. I had to follow up later and apologize, then explain my *real* (curious, not judgmental) intention and communicate differently.

The lesson? What you *think* you're saying isn't always what someone else is hearing. Be mindful of how your words might land, regardless of your intent.

The Bottom Line: Engage with Purpose

Ultimately, meaningful engagement doesn't come from a script or a pitch or hustling to get more face time. It comes from curiosity and conversation.

This is how moments get made. Listening. Pausing. Responding thoughtfully. Being curious. Communicating clearly and effectively. Just think for a moment what your life would be like if everyone in it did this. It's a nice image, right?

When you master real, purposeful engagement, you move beyond transactions and start building real relationships and making moments that matter.

Espresso Shot: Your Challenge

Starting now, write "STAY CURIOUS" at the top of your notes or agenda heading into a meeting and see what you can discover.

CHAPTER 9

What About ______?— Navigating the Unexpected

Alright, we've journeyed through the core of the BREW Method. But let's be real. Life doesn't always follow the plan.

You can be prepared, create the structure, show up with confidence, and then...bam. The unexpected happens. The client throws you a curveball. Technology implodes. The meeting setting changes. Just fill in the blank.

One of the clients I coached encountered a real "What About ______?". He had prepped meticulously for a three-minute segment as part of a much larger presentation. And he was ready—structure in place—focused on intention, and ready to tackle it with impact. Then, on the day, the entire format shifted.

He was told that he was now covering the topic during a lunch with key stakeholders. Suddenly, all of the variables were completely different. The three minutes he had prepped for now became 45. And to top it all off, he was now presenting during lunch (and who LOVES listening to a presentation during lunch? Nobody.) His initial reaction? Panic. His perfect plan was useless. He felt like he'd lost all control.

This is the W of BREW. It's the moment you think, "What the...?!" or "What was that?" It's the blank space in your plan you didn't see coming. This chapter is about answering the question: What About _______? (Insert your unexpected scenario here). It's about how you pivot, adapt, and even find opportunity when things go sideways.

Embracing the "Blank": Your Mindset for the Unexpected

What happens when your plan evaporates? Do you have a full-blown meltdown? Do you let your momentum crumble and phone it all in? No. You shift your mindset. You stop fighting the unexpected and start to lean into it, maybe even have a little fun with it.

This is the beauty of the BREW Method. Everything I covered in the last several chapters matters. All of the tips and suggestions are valuable. And at the end of the day, it's the philosophy behind each step that matters most, not exactly how it plays out.

For example, you need structure and intention for momentum. The checklist of ways to make that happen? Less important than the overall goal: to step up, be the moment, and lead the interaction. If your agenda somehow disappeared and your presentation stopped working, you could still fall back on your intention and your structure, leading the conversation to the CTA.

This is a lesson that paid off for a client of mine who was preparing for a presentation and he had a feeling that something was "off." The people in charge of the setup weren't getting back to him. He was feeling like something was going to go wrong.

I told him, "Prepare for the shit. Prepare for it to go wrong." He practiced his presentation. He focused on remembering the most important information that he wanted to get across. He structured his talking points in advance.

And sure enough, when he showed up, the "what if" happened. His clicker wouldn't work, so the slides wouldn't advance. The setting turned out to be different than what he'd pictured. And his topic wasn't completely aligned with the audience.

Instead of panicking, he leaned back on everything he'd prepared. He knew what he was going to say, even without his slides. He held himself confidently. He focused on connecting with the audience through eye contact and engagement. And his presentation turned out to be a big success.

You have to prepare for the messy. Things change. The unexpected happens. If you've prepared and planned, you set yourself up for success anyway.

Let's look at some other examples of handling the "What if" in action:

What if…the agenda gets hijacked? Acknowledge the new direction. "It sounds like X is really important to discuss right now." If possible, try to subtly link it back to your overall objective or suggest how you can incorporate it. "Great, let's dive into X. Perhaps we can explore how that connects to [original objective]."

What if……you're asked a question you can't answer? Don't bluff. It's okay not to know everything. "That's an excellent question, and I want to make sure I give you the most accurate information. Let me look into that and get back to you by [specific time/date]."

What if…someone is clearly disengaged or hostile? Don't ignore it, but don't get defensive. Try a gentle engagement. "David, I notice you've been quiet. What are your initial thoughts on this?" Or, if appropriate, address the perceived concern calmly: "It seems like there might be some reservations about X. Can we talk through those?"

What if…the internet goes down or a tech problem happens? If you're prepared, and confident in what you're saying (and why you're saying it), you can lean back on your talking points—the technology isn't what creates connection, you are.

What if…something embarrassing happens? Use it. Own it. Call it out. I recently had a lunch meeting with the head of HR for a major company, feeling very put together in my crisp white blazer. One enthusiastic dip of bread later, and my sleeve was swimming in tomato soup.

Of course, she was the one to notice and point it out to me. And I was conducting a training for the company immediately following the meeting.

She was incredibly gracious—trying to help me blot it out, then calling her assistant to hunt down a stain-remover pen. At one point she was literally holding my arm and scrubbing my sleeve like I was a 5-year-old who'd just come in from recess. There's nothing quite like sitting across from a senior leader while she circles a Tide pen on your outfit.

Unfortunately, it was the kind of stain that was not coming off easily. I had to step in front of a room of people ready to learn from me, soup blazer and all. Not my finest wardrobe moment.

So I walked into the training room, 40 people looking at me, feeling like the orange stain on my sleeve was shining out like a beacon.

What did I do? I owned it.

I opened the session with:

"Before we begin—yes, the tomato soup is delicious, and yes, I'm apparently wearing it today."

The room laughed. The tension dropped. And we got on with it.

The lesson? When the _______ happens, don't sweat it. In fact, use it or call it out if you can. Life can throw curveballs at you any time. Embarrassing moments will happen. You get to choose how you respond to them. (And if you get the chance to laugh at yourself, take it. Humor creates engagement and makes you memorable.)

Embrace Your Weird (and Theirs)

Sometimes the unexpected is just...awkward. You say something that lands weird, or they do. Someone makes an odd comment. Instead of cringing or trying to smooth it over instantly, just own it. Embrace the weird. If you stumble over a word or have an awkward moment, acknowledge it, and laugh along at yourself. It shows you're human.

And when your client brings the weird, get curious about it instead of letting it throw you. Remember, everyone is Human: That "bigwig" CEO who just derailed your agenda with an off-topic question? Human. That prospect who seems completely disengaged? Human. That panelist who just said something that seems completely irrelevant? Human.

When you remember that everyone in the room is just a person, with their own pressures, quirks, and off days, it de-escalates the pressure you put on yourself. Things get messy because people are messy. That's the beauty in human connection.

You never know when the weird moments are going to give you the most real connections and conversations. Don't shy away from the weird. Let it in.

Be flexible. Be curious. Be open to the unexpected. Be willing to move with the environment, not against it.

Part 2 Reflection: Learning from the Moment Makers

We've reached the end of part 2 and the core of the BREW Method. Next, you'll learn how to put it into action in specific workplace scenarios. As you start to practice these elements, I want to leave you with one final thought for this section: Become an observer of masterful moment makers.

BECOME AN OBSERVER OF MASTERFUL MOMENT MAKERS.

Presence, confidence, engagement, and adaptability aren't abstract theories; you see them in action every day if you look for them.

Think about people you admire, not just in business but in life: leaders in your industry, compelling public figures, inspiring historical characters, well-written characters in books or movies, or even everyday people around you that you interact with every day.

How do they handle unexpected challenges? How do they command a room with quiet confidence? How do they hold their bodies or communicate nonverbally? How do they make others feel truly heard and understood? How do they pivot gracefully when things don't go as planned? What can you learn from them?

You can find moment makers in line at the grocery store or sitting in the chair next to you while you're getting a haircut or sitting around at a coffee shop. When you start paying attention, you'll notice them.

Pay attention to the moment makers. Learn from them. And remember that these are skills you can practice and build over time. The world is full of teachers if you're open to learning.

Espresso Shot: Your Challenge

The unexpected is guaranteed. Your response is your choice. What ONE small mindset shift or tactic from this chapter can you commit to practicing when faced with a minor "blank" this week? Pick one to practice:

- Consciously "lean into" a slightly awkward moment instead of avoiding it.
- When a plan changes, ask a clarifying question before reacting.
- Remind yourself "everyone is human" when someone acts unexpectedly.
- Intentionally observe one person navigating an unexpected situation and note what you learn.

Create the Moment

CHAPTER 10

Prospecting

W elcome to part 3! We've laid the groundwork with the philosophies behind the BREW Method (to recap: Be the Moment, Raise Confidence, Engage, and What About _______?).

It's time to learn how these each apply to every part your sales process:

- Prospecting
- Networking (and all its variations)
- Meetings
- Presentations
- Follow-up
- Negotiating

In part 3, each chapter will walk you through how the BREW Method can be applied to these areas, with concrete examples and action plans.

Let's start with prospecting, one of the most universally hated parts of the job. If the mere mention of prospecting makes you want to conveniently "forget" to open your CRM, you're not alone. But you can BREW successful prospecting to create momentum in a way that doesn't feel sleazy.

B: Be the Moment in Momentum—Building Intention and Structure Into Prospecting

We all know prospecting is a big part of the job. Why the universal dread? Psychologically, it's tough. We're reaching out to people we don't know. We're worried about bothering people. We often don't know what to say, so we default to pitching.

And that uncertainty, that discomfort? It comes from not having a plan. Without structure and intention, you're almost guaranteed to fall back into old patterns that get you ghosted.

Let's do it differently.

Setting Your Intention

Let's get one thing straight: The purpose of prospecting is not to close the deal on the spot. You're not trying to sell them today. You're trying to spark curiosity, create awareness, and begin building presence in their world. You want them to know who you are and why you're worth paying attention to.

Here's how *not to do that*: launching into a cold pitch all about you, you, you. That's the fastest way to get ignored in a B2B environment where every executive's inbox is already overflowing with "let me tell you about my company" emails, most of which get ignored.

Instead, focus on how to make your pitch *relevant to the prospect*. Be a resource, not a megaphone. This comes from doing your homework. Yes, I know you've been told this before. Yes, I know it's obvious. We're all told to research and personalize our outreach. We're not taught how to actually do it.

BE A RESOURCE, NOT A MEGAPHONE.

What should we find out? And how can you use that information effectively? Start by thinking beyond the obvious (their title or how long they've been in business).

Are they active on LinkedIn? Are they posting interesting content you can talk about? Did their company win any recent awards or go through an acquisition? Were they in the press recently?

Then, take that information and use it to personalize your outreach. That doesn't mean congratulate them briefly on a win and then jump into your pitch. It means use that information to actually offer something of value.

Find a golden nugget and ask yourself how you can help support them in what they're doing. That's what you reach out with.

Brew It Better	
Instead of this…	Try this…
"Hi Sarah, My name is Amy with ProjectFlow, and our platform helps marketing teams like yours streamline their workflows and increase productivity. I'd love to schedule 15 minutes to show you a demo." "Hi David, I saw your company was recently acquired and wanted to tell you about our integration software. We help businesses merge their tech stacks seamlessly after a merger."	"Hi Sarah, your recent LinkedIn post about the challenge of scaling content production while maintaining brand voice really resonated. That's a tough balancing act many leaders face during a growth phase. I had a quick thought on how other teams are tackling this that you might find interesting." "Hi David, congratulations on the recent acquisition! That's a huge milestone. I know from experience that the process of integrating two different tech stacks can be a massive operational lift. I recently put together a brief checklist on the 'First 90 Days of Post-Acquisition System Integration'—thought you might find it useful as you navigate this transition."

Which one sounds generic? Which one would *you* be more likely to respond to? It's no contest.

And what if you can't find any recent news or LinkedIn content? Personalize it as best as you can. Try something like: "Hi [name], reaching out because I know you lead the operations team at your company. I work with operations leaders in the tech space and one theme I'm seeing this year is the difficulty of maintaining project velocity as teams and workflows become more complex. Wondering how your team is navigating that particular challenge. Curious to see if you would like to get on a 15-minute call to discuss how that's going for you today."

In this case, you're still not pitching. You're explaining why you're asking for the time and extending an invitation to talk so you can learn more about their world.

Blind Prospecting vs. Targeted Prospecting: Getting Intentional

Not all prospecting is created equal. In the sales world, outreach generally falls into two distinct categories: blind prospecting and targeted prospecting.

Blind is likely what you think of when you imagine a classic, high-volume sales floor. It starts with an engineered list, a massive database of contacts, often purchased from a third party or generated by a system. This list is dumped into a CRM, and then a generic marketing campaign is pushed out to everyone on it.

It's a blind campaign built on the numbers game: If you send out thousands of emails, a small fraction will inevitably respond. There's little personalization and minimal research. Can it generate activity? Sure. Does it lead to connection and momentum? Sometimes. Blind campaigns have their place: to get in front of people and hopefully get noticed. Most of your focus needs to go into targeted prospecting though.

It's different, more intentional. You might start with that same large list of 200 viable companies in your territory, but instead of hitting "send all," you start scrubbing.

You become a strategist. You identify the high-potential accounts, looking for connections, like a potential referral you could leverage. You prioritize based on strategic fit and your own research. From that list of 200, you curate your top 50, or even your top 20, and devise a personalized plan to engage *them*.

You research their challenges, understand who you're reaching out to, and build value into your outreach. Essentially, it's "you framing" your prospecting.

Blind prospecting has its place. But when we talk about brewing momentum, we're focusing on targeted outreach, where you can create meaningful moments.

Personalize, Don't Pitch

Prospecting is a numbers game, to be sure. However, it's more complex than just churning out calls. *Gong* conducted a study on cold-calling that showed there's more to it than the numbers. The average sales rep received a 27% open rate to cold outreach and a 15% rate of converting prospects to meetings. But top performers had a much different result: a 58% open rate and a 27% meeting conversion rate.[23]

What can we learn from that study? What you say in your outreach has a big impact. And if you can learn how to become one of the top performers, you're going to be playing a much stronger numbers game.

Fun fact: That same study showed that one of the biggest factors that led to *less successful* outreach was pitching. When reps pitched in their email outreach, it led to a *57% lower response rate.* When outreach skipped a hard pitch and instead focused on language and examples that were *personal* to the prospect, the response rates were significantly better.[24]

The big lesson here? *Relevance is better than volume.* A pitch-heavy email sent thousands of times won't be as powerful as a well-crafted personal message sent hundreds of times. The bottom line? Your outreach needs to be intentional.

For the record, I'm not advocating for a two-page email drafted specifically for your prospect (in fact, please don't send that.) However, there's a balance between numbers and personalization. You can keep things simple and replicable and still prioritize personal connection. (We'll talk more about what to say in your outreach when we get to E: Engagement.)

---

23 Gong, "Does Cold Email Even Work Anymore?" *LinkedIn Pulse*, accessed August 4, 2025, https://www.linkedin.com/pulse/does-cold-email-even-work-anymore-gong-io-vlj1e/.

24 Gong, "Does Cold Email Even Work Anymore?"

Structuring Your Cadence

The other biggest piece to structure in prospecting is your outreach cadence—how many times you'll attempt to connect, what methods you'll use (call, email, LinkedIn, video, etc.), and at what time intervals. Most salespeople track this through a CRM. (You *can* use an Excel spreadsheet, but honestly, I don't advise it if you want to scale or stay sane.)

Now for the hard truth of this hard skill set: 60% of prospects say no (or simply don't respond) at least *four times* before they might engage or say yes.[25] This means for true cold outreach, you need a cadence with *at least six touchpoints*.

What?! That seems like a lot. I hear this all the time. We might feel comfortable following up once or twice, but beyond that we think we're bothering people or we don't know what else to say.

The statistics don't lie though. Giving up after one or two is just leaving opportunity on the table. And the more frequent your touchpoints are *on the front end* of your cadence, the higher your overall response rate will likely be. Yes, that's when it feels most awkward. It's also when it's the most important.

You also need to consider your method of outreach. Calls are statistically shown to be more effective, again and again. In a B2B setting, cold calls have a 5% higher response rate than cold emails.[26] That doesn't mean toss email out. It means to do both.

---

25 "60% of customers say no four times before saying yes." SalesLion, accessed August 16, 2025, https://saleslion.io/sales-statistics/60-of-customers-say-no-four-times-before-saying-yes/.

26 Rachana Pallikaraki, "Cold Calling vs Cold Emailing in 2025: The Ultimate Sales Showdown," Martal Solutions, February 26, 2025, https://martal.ca/cold-calling-vs-cold-emailing-lb/.

Call first, then email. A hybrid approach leads to 4.7 times more prospect engagement.[27] (And don't forget other methods, like LinkedIn DMs, other relevant social platforms, texts, or even personalized video messages. Strategic incorporation of these is part of your plan.)

A basic, high-impact starting cadence:

- Day 1, Touchpoint 1 (Call): Call your prospect. If they answer, great! If not, leave a clear, concise voicemail stating *briefly* why you're calling and letting them know an email with more context is coming their way immediately. You need to write this out loud and practice it. How many times have you rambled on a voicemail? Stop doing that.
- Day 1, Touchpoint 2 (Email): Send that email right after the call. The subject line and content should align directly with your voicemail message. (Boom – two touchpoints, same day, reinforcing your message).
- Day 2 or 3, Touchpoint 3 (LinkedIn/Social or other): Connect on LinkedIn with a personalized note. Or, depending on the prospect and your research, perhaps another brief email with a relevant article or insight. (Note how within just two days, you've already had *three* touchpoints. They can become more spaced out over time.)
- Day 5, Touchpoint 4: Call and leave a voicemail.
- Day 7, Touchpoint 5: Send a video or message on LinkedIn
- Day 8, Touchpoint 6: Call and leave a voicemail.

---

27 Pallikaraki, "Cold Calling vs Cold Emailing in 2025: The Ultimate Sales Showdown."

- Day 10, Touchpoint 7: Engage with content on LinkedIn again.
- Day 15, Touchpoint 8: Email them again and let them know what to expect next from you.

Remember, this is just one example. Beyond the first call and the initial follow-up email, make it your own; just keep the frequency up. Also, keep in mind that this cadence is for initial, cold outreach. If you get a response at any point, your outreach naturally shifts from "prospecting cadence" to "active follow-up and engagement," which we'll go into in chapter 16.

R: Raise Your Prospecting Confidence

Prospecting can be a confidence-killer. That fear of rejection, of bothering someone, of not knowing what to say: it's why many salespeople delay outreach or give up too soon.

Fortunately, there are ways to raise your confidence when prospecting. The truth is that your structure alone will give you a lot of confidence. When you have a plan in place for how often to reach out, you don't have to debate with yourself. That feeling of seemingly bothering prospects by reaching out again a day or two after your first attempt? That's your lack of confidence talking, not a reflection of their annoyance. I say this with love—get over it. Get out of your own way.

There's a psychological effect that happens when we are repeatedly seen called *priming bias*. This is what occurs when our brain is more likely to notice and remember something we've already interacted with multiple times. It's why billboards and commercials have been effective for years. If you've heard a brand's name multiple times, you're going to remember them when you need a product or service. We're more likely to purchase from someone we're *already familiar with*.

When we put ourselves in front of our prospects repeatedly, we're activating priming bias. Instead of worrying about "bothering" them, remember that your intention is to get noticed and make sure you get remembered.

It's also to *add value.* If you're taking away the generic pitch and genuinely trying to offer solutions for clients, you don't need to worry about "bothering" them. Reframe it: You're not trying to "sell them." You're trying to help them solve their problems.

And if you still find yourself struggling with confidence when it comes to outreach, practice it until you become it.

Power pose before you send a call. Practice your voicemails. Push yourself through the uncomfortable. Yes, it's going to be uncomfortable at first. That discomfort will fade over time. Keep on practicing. Stick to your cadence. And raise your confidence, one outreach at a time.

E: Engage—Making Every Contact Count

With your plan in place and your confidence bolstered, it's time to actually communicate. The E: Engage in prospecting comes into play with how you word your emails, structure your voicemails, and personalize your DMs.

Voicemails (That Won't Get Immediately Ignored)

Here's how a typical cold voicemail goes:

"Hi [Prospect Name], this is [Your Name] from [Your Company]. We specialize in [services/products]...I'd love to schedule some time...Please call me back..."

Yawn. It's all about you. There's nothing personal. You sound like every one of your competitors. And you've really given them NO reason to call you back or keep you on their radar.

So…what would a voicemail look like the BREW way? Let's reframe it to create impact:

Brew It Better	
Instead of this…	Try this…
"Hi [Prospect Name), this is Amy Reczek with Sales & Presence. We specialize in helping companies like yours train their teams for more effective sales. Call me back."	""Hi [Prospect Name], this is Amy Reczek with Sales & Presence. I realize you weren't expecting my call, so I'll keep it short. I'm sending over a quick email with an idea I thought might be useful, especially given [reference something specific you researched, like their recent training initiatives]. No need to return this call unless it hits the mark—the email will include my direct contact info. Again, this is Amy Reczek with Sales & Presence. Wishing you a productive day."

See the difference? First, it acknowledges the interruption right away. This creates a psychological effect; the prospect recognizes and appreciates that you are being respectful of their time. Then, it focuses on the prospect instead of a pitch, offering value. Finally, it directs them to an easy next step (the email).

Emails Worth Opening and Reading

Calls are important, but let's not forget emails—you need to use both together to frontload your touchpoints when prospecting. The average person receives 121 emails a day.[28] How are you going to stand out?

Hook Them With Your Subject Line

One of the first shifts to make in prospecting? Write better email subject lines. Studies show that over 40% of people open an email based on the subject line alone.[29] If yours is boring, generic, or self-serving, you've lost the game before it even starts.

What's the typical, ineffective subject line we see all the time? Something like, [My Company] + [Their Company] or Introduction from Sales & Presence. It's bland, it screams "SALES PITCH," and it's practically begging to be dragged into the trash folder.

---

28 Shubham Singh, "How Many Emails Are Sent Per Day? (2025 Statistics)," Demand Sage, accessed April 17, 2025, https://www.demandsage.com/how-many-emails-are-sent-per-day/.

29 Doug Bonderud, "30+ Statistics About Sales Email Subject Lines You Need to Know," HubSpot Blog, May 22, 2025, https://blog.hubspot.com/sales/subject-line-stats-open-rates-slideshare.

Let's be different. One powerful way to do this is to tap into a psychological trigger: curiosity and the fear of missing out (FOMO). For a cold outreach, try a subject line like:

Subject line: Connecting Tuesday, June 25th at 10:00 a.m.

What happened when you read that? When a prospect sees this in their inbox, they have a human reaction. They think, "Wait, what's happening on the 25th? Am I supposed to know about this? Did I miss something?" It creates a tiny, urgent information gap that they feel compelled to close by clicking "open." That's why this is my personal favorite.

Here are a few other subject lines that feel different and pique interest:

- [Mutual acquaintance] suggested I get in touch with you
- Ideas for [topic prospect cares about]
- Question about [goal]
- This is a sales email

That last one feels funny, but it works. Just like the BREW voicemail, acknowledging the elephant in the room puts prospects at ease and makes them curious to see what else you're going to say.

Keep the Momentum Going

You created an engaging subject line. Now what? In the body, keep the focus on your prospect, offer value, and form a connection.

How can you do that? Keep your email to a few short sentences centered on:

- The reason you're reaching out
- The problem your prospect is facing
- What value you can offer

Here's an example of what that might look like:

Hi Susan,

Your agency's recent LinkedIn post about "investing in technology to streamline the broker experience" caught my attention.

Empowering producers is a challenge, especially when the manual data entry for complex commercial quotes can consume so much of their day.

We're helping another regional brokerage reduce their quoting time by over 30%, allowing their team to spend more time advising clients and less on paperwork.

It's short, sweet, and to the point and can lead right into your structured close.

Close with a Strong CTA

Your email outreach needs to end with a strong and clear CTA. Remember, it's not just a call to action; it's also the confidence to act. You want to give the other person the confidence to want to take an action. How? By being confident yourself and giving them a clear next step.

If this resonates with you…I'd love to connect for a 10-minute conversation. How does [date/time] look for you?

Excited to chat and spark some ideas together!

It creates a specific next step, gives them an easy way to accept or decline, and closes with confidence.

Let's put all of that together and brew it better. Here's an example of a typical cold email:

Hi Debbie,

My name is Amy and I am the founder of Sales and Presence, a company that helps sales teams become more efficient by focusing on power skills.

I just wanted to reach out because I will be in Dallas next week speaking at a conference and I hoped that I would have the opportunity to meet with you while I'm in town.

I have noticed some trends regarding nonverbal communication in sales. I think your team might find this info helpful. Maybe we could meet to talk through them?

I help companies like yours at Sales and Presence, but before I started the company I also worked in corporate sales for 17 years and have seen firsthand how the strategies we teach can help sales reps build more confidence and close more sales.

Would you maybe be interested in chatting?

Wishing you well,

Amy

Where did this go wrong? Let's break it down:

- It's all about ME from the very beginning. "I, my, I'm…."
- It uses A LOT of words that diminish which come across as weak and unconfident. (Can you find them? *I just*

wanted to...I think your team might find...Would you maybe...? Maybe we could meet...)

- And it leaves the ball completely in the other person's court, forcing them to look at their calendar and respond back with suggested times if they're interested. Never make them work! Do the heavy lifting for them.

Even just a slight reframe can make this significantly stronger.

Hi Debbie,

Hope the week is off to a strong start.

After reviewing [company name], there are some compelling insights worth sharing around how nonverbal communication can directly impact closing rates. With a background in corporate sales, there's relevant experience and strategies that could be valuable to your team.

Coming to Dallas next week to speak at a conference—it's a great opportunity to connect while in town.

Are you open for a quick 30 min conversation on Thursday May 20th at 11:30 or 3:00?

Looking forward to the conversation,

Amy

This second version isn't drastically different from the first one. It contains most of the same basic information with the same request. But the changes are powerful.

First, the greeting. "Hope all is well" is a strong opener, even if it feels like it's "empty language." In fact, emails that contain the phrase "hope all is well" currently show a 24% increase in response rate.[30] That might change, and it's important to keep up on the current trends. For now, *hope all is well* is a win. And if it *feels* empty or inauthentic, tweak it slightly by adding "at the start of the week" or "heading into a long weekend" to add a specific, genuine touchpoint.

Then, I jump right into talking about the prospect's company and the value I want to offer, just hinting slightly at why I'm worth listening to, "you framing" instead of focusing on myself.

Finally, I give two clear options for a meeting and sign off with confidence.

DMs (LinkedIn, etc.) & Texts: Connection First

Nobody, I repeat NOBODY likes a pitchy first DM. Let's toss that out right now. Your first message should always be about connection, not a sales pitch.

For example:

"Hi [Prospect Name], I saw your recent article on [topic]. Great insights on [specific point]. Would love to connect and follow your work."

Keep it targeted, specific, and intentional. The goal is to open a door, not force a sale.

Video Messaging: The Impact of Visuals:

Video is a huge opportunity. You've probably heard the statistics: Sales teams that use video in their outreach see a

---

30 Gong, "'HOPE ALL IS WELL' Personally, we hate it. It's trite and outdated and the opposite of personal. But what if you could say something different in your cold emails to stand out?," LinkedIn, https://www.linkedin.com/posts/gong-io_hope-all-is-well-personally-we-hate-activity-7279519458233131008-Iuit.

16% increase in open rates and a 26% increase in replies.[31] And yet, time and time again, I've encouraged the sales teams I train to employ it, and time and time again, they haven't. I've even suggested that they use me to practice. They very rarely do. This is one of those times when you need to push yourself through the discomfort wall.

Maybe video isn't for you (although it's a valuable chance to stand out, so I encourage you to explore it.) If not, find a way to make yourself stand out and be different.

W: What About ______?—When Your Prospecting Hits a Snag

Even with the best plan, confidence, and engagement skills, prospecting has its "What about ______?" moments. For this chapter, let's keep it simple and focus on the most common one:

What if...they don't respond after your full initial cadence?

This is where many salespeople throw in the towel. Don't. "No response" means "no right now," not "no forever."

As much as we would all love it if our clients were always on our timeline, that's not always the case. Some clients are "not now" clients. Think about it—you are reaching out to them on a random Tuesday to connect. You have no idea what is happening in their world—new boss, travel, onboarding new team members, acquisition, start of school, hard life things— the list is endless.

---

31 Kendall Walters, "Video Prospecting for Sales: How to Use Video to Book More Meetings," Vidyard, July 14, 2023. https://www.vidyard.com/blog/video-prospecting/.

If you've followed up and haven't heard anything, smoothly transition the prospect from your active prospecting cadence to your long-term, low-touch quarterly nurture plan (remember, you still want to be activating priming bias and staying in front of your prospects.) Send a valuable article, industry insight, or relevant company news every few months.

Espresso Shot: Your Challenge

Incorporate a short, personalized video in your next cold email outreach. Keep it under 60 seconds, be yourself, mention something specific to them, and offer a clear, low-pressure next step.

Summary: BREW in Prospecting

B: Be the Moment

- Reframe your intention. It's *not* to make an immediate sale. Your true intention is to get their interest and build familiarity/activate priming bias.
- Personalize, don't pitch. Research and identify your ideal prospect and find a way to offer them value.
- Build your cadence. Structure a sequence of at least six touchpoints, frontloaded as much as possible.

R: Raise Confidence

- Get out of your own way. Waiting a week to follow up isn't being polite; it's a sign of *your* lack of confidence.
- Reframe it. You're not trying to "sell them." You're trying to help them solve their problems.

- Practice until you become it. If making calls or sending videos feels uncomfortable, practice! Power pose before you dial. Rehearse your voicemails. Discomfort fades with practice.

E: Engage

- Call first, then email.
- Reframe your voicemails to do the following:
  » Acknowledge the unexpected call ("I know you weren't expecting my call...").
  » Focus on *their* world by referencing something specific you researched.
  » Direct them to an easy next step (like the email you're about to send).
- Keep emails concise, focus on the value you can offer *them*, and use "You framing" instead of "I framing."
- Use DMs & texts for connection first, not sales pitches. Reference a shared interest or their recent activity to open a door.
- Use video to stand out and create a powerful visual connection. Keep it brief (under 60 seconds) and authentic.

W: What About _______? (When Prospecting Hits a Wall)

- *What if...they don't respond after your full cadence?* Don't delete them or keep hammering them with the same ask. This means "no *right now*," not "no forever. Transition them from your active prospecting list to a long-term, low-touch quarterly nurture plan.

CHAPTER 11

Networking (Conferences, Happy Hours, Etc.)

Moving on to networking! What do you think of when you hear the word? Awkward small talk at a conference? A happy hour with forced conversation? Golf?

It's all networking, and it's all unfortunately a missed opportunity all too often. Just like with prospecting, the biggest reason why is a "wing it and hope for the best" mentality. Without a plan in place, you probably find yourself glued to your phone pretending to be busy, making a beeline for the bar as a safety net, or only talking to the handful of people you already know.

I used to be the queen of this. It's common: Go attend! Mingle! Build relationships! What a bunch of shit. It's *exhausting*. The number one response I get when asking teams how they feel about networking is, "It's a lot." And it is. It takes a lot of your time, energy, and effort. Don't get me wrong, networking is great. I always say "out of the office is where deals are closed" but not if we are just showing up with no direction.

If this is your typical networking experience, you're missing out on prime opportunities to create real moments and build powerful momentum. But it doesn't have to be that way. Great networking—like great coffee—is all about the blend: bold, warm, and again, intentional.

Let's learn how to flip the script and apply the BREW Method to make your networking more intentional, impactful, and maybe even enjoyable.

B: Be the Moment in Networking—Creating Momentum With Structure

Too many people wander into networking events like they're just taking a walk: no plan, no real purpose, hoping something good might randomly happen. That's not a strategy; that's leaving connection and momentum entirely to chance.

Instead, let's get deliberate, starting with defining your intention and then building a smart structure around it.

Setting Your Networking Intention: Warming the Mug

Just like you wouldn't pour espresso into a cold mug, don't walk into a room cold. Get intentional. Know what energy you're bringing and why you're there. What's your actual intention for this networking event? If your first thought is "to get leads" or "to close deals," hit the brakes.

You need to focus on curiosity, connection, and exploration. For example, your intention might be to have a few authentic conversations where you actually learn something about the other person. Or it might be to discover if there's a potential alignment of interests, needs, or opportunities. Maybe it's to collect business cards from three quality connections. It can even be to create the next small step, like setting up a coffee meet-up. But whatever it is, it's not a sale. (Remember, brewing takes time!)

Building Your Networking Structure (Your Plan of Attack to Ditch the Safety Nets)

With your intention clear, now you build a structure to support it. This starts with putting in prep before the event.

First, and *obviously*, do your homework. I shouldn't even have to tell you this one. If there's an attendee list, a conference app, or speakers you can research, do it. Identify a few people or companies you'd ideally like to connect with. What are they working on? What can you say that's more memorable than, "So…what do you do?"

Next, think about your game plan for the event itself and how you're going to create momentum, starting with how you're going to move through the room. If you're at a conference with a booth, plan to, at the very least, stand in front of it (think back to Starbucks Kid and how he removed the barrier, creating more connection with everyone in the coffee shop).

When you're not at a booth, what are you going to be doing? Heading to a session? Visiting other booths? Chatting with attendees?

As you engage, be listening for opportunities to naturally suggest a follow-up (we'll cover the how of that engagement in the 'E' section).

Remember that your structure isn't just for formal conferences. Whether it's a formal conference, a casual happy hour, a golf outing, or even client pedicures, your intention and structure still need to be in place. Know your intention and head in with a plan.

> **KNOW YOUR INTENTION AND HEAD IN WITH A PLAN.**

R: Raise Confidence for Networking—Owning Your Presence

Now, let's talk confidence. How are you going to stand out from everyone else? How are you going to be memorable? By *owning your presence*.

This starts with the basics. Remember that your nonverbal actions are 93% of how you communicate. You're "talking" loudly when you enter a room, before you even say a word.

Before you enter any networking room, walk yourself through a quick mental check on your nonverbal communication:

- Hands: Visible and ready to gesture naturally or offer a handshake (phone put away)
- Posture: Open, tall, shoulders back
- Eyes: Alert and ready to make genuine eye contact

Remember that even when you've prepped, even when you've power posed, even when your physical presence is firing on all cylinders and you've dressed for success and you're ready to roll, it might still feel awkward to start conversations. Everyone feels it. The confidence comes from knowing it's normal and doing it anyway, armed with your structured plan in place.

The other piece of confidence in networking is playing to your strengths. That starts with understanding who you are. Some people are over-the-top extroverts who *love* walking into a new room and meeting people. If that's not you, trying to force yourself to become that person is likely to backfire. You'll get more exhausted, feel more awkward, and end up coming across as inauthentic or unengaged.

Instead, play to your strengths. There are different ways to be a successful networker. After watching and observing what makes for successful networking, I've carved out five "Presence Profiles." Each of these has strengths that can lead to strong connections:

The Strategist

These are the people who analyze every move, think before they speak, and can articulate their viewpoints with crystal clarity. If you're a Strategist, you likely have valuable insight to add. You approach networking strategically, thinking about how many people you want to talk to or what types of connections you're hoping to make.

You can thrive in networking by offering impact and insight into conversations, making you a memorable connection.

However, if you're not careful, you'll end up overthinking or missing moments because you're in your head trying to plan out how to articulate your thoughts.

The Observer

Like Strategists, Observers tend to be more quiet; but instead of thinking about their next move or planning what to say, they're focused on noticing other people. They're perceptive and pick up on things easily, which is a big advantage.

If you're an Observer, use those observations to connect with people. Don't let yourself fall through the cracks or forget to interject and engage with others.

The Bridge Builder

You know those people who seem to know everything about everyone, in a good way? I like to call them Bridge Builders—they connect people together and have a knack for finding common ground between others. If you're more of an Observer or a Strategist, Bridge Builders need to be your best friend at a networking event. They can help you connect easily—and are more than happy to do so.

If you're a Bridge Builder, watch out for overexerting yourself or doing too much for others. It's great to connect people, but remember to focus on what you need from an event as well.

The Anchor

Anchors are the reliable, steady ones—people you can count on to provide a rational viewpoint on any topic and keep a conversation grounded. They make you feel calmer just by their presence and ease.

If you're an Anchor, just make sure your calmness isn't being perceived as aloofness. You need to let people know that you are engaged and interested in what they have to say.

The Spark

When we think of networking events, we all know that person who buzzes from group to group seamlessly or ends up having a group gather around them with ease. They're never the ones standing on the sideline, gearing themselves up to go talk to someone. I call them "Sparks" because they light up the room.

Networking might feel more natural to Sparks; but if this is you, you also need to be cautious of overpowering conversations. Make sure you're still having meaningful communication and listening to other people.

Presence Profiles			
	Description	Strengths	Watch out for...
The Strategist	Thoughtful, intentional, and calculated in your presence. You observe before you engage, and when you speak, it's impactful.	Insightful, articulate, planned	Overthinking, hesitating too long to jump in

The Observer	Quietly powerful. Observers take everything in, often noticing dynamics others miss. When you speak, it's intentional and insightful.	Perceptive, reflective, intentional	Being overlooked, not voicing valuable insights
The Bridge Builder	Natural connector who brings people together. You excel at finding common ground and creating shared understanding.	Empathetic, collaborative, inclusive	People-pleasing, spreading yourself too thin
The Anchor	Calm, steady, and grounded. You provide stability and confidence in group dynamics—you bring weight and presence without demanding attention.	Reliable, composed, confident	Appearing aloof or too reserved
The Spark	Charismatic, energetic, and instantly engaging. You light up a room and attract others with enthusiasm and openness.	Inspiring, approachable, energizing	Overshadowing others, speaking more than listening

(Curious about your networking profile? Check the Resources section of the book for a link to a quiz to find out which you lean toward.)

Using Profiles to Your Advantage

When you understand your strengths, you can use them more effectively. If you're not an Anchor or a Bridge Builder, you don't need to try to talk to every single person in the room. A few quality connections can be just as effective.

If you are an Anchor or a Bridge Builder, use that strength. Meet more people and let yourself quickly identify the people you could potentially build stronger relationships with.

Spend some time thinking about where you fall and what you can do with your strengths. And start paying attention to other people around you and identifying where they fall—this will help you know how to engage better with everyone. If you notice that someone is an Observer, ask them for an insight. For a Strategist, talk with them about their plans for the next month or quarter. People will feel seen and appreciated when you tap into what makes them tick.

Remember that your profile isn't "fixed." You might feel more like a Bridge Builder one day, but when you're drained at the end of the week, you might be more of an Anchor. Before heading into an event, tune into yourself and think about where you fall. Instead of fighting against yourself, be aware of potential pitfalls but head in leading with your strengths.

E: Engage in Networking—Stirring Real Conversations

You've prepped, you're present, you're aware of your strengths, you're feeling confident. Now it's time to actually engage, to connect beyond superficial small talk.

This starts with your opening. How many of you lead with, "So, what do you do?" And how many times have you heard somebody else lead with the exact same question? Safe? Yes. Habit? Yes. Memorable? NO.

It's just like asking your partner, "How was your day?" or asking a child, "How was school? What did you do?" What kind of answers do you get to these questions? One word, automatic answers: Fine, good, okay, nothing. No real engagement, no momentum for more conversation.

Instead, let's think back to curiosity. Look around your environment and think about what unique conversation starters you can use. One of my favorites is something like "Hi, I'm Amy. That cocktail looks amazing…is it your go-to drink?"

Another great way to create engagement is to ask open-ended questions that invite more than a one-word response:

"This is my first time at this conference…do you come here a lot? What's the most valuable part to you?"

"What's been your favorite takeaway from the session so far?"

"What has been exciting about this quarter for you and your team?"

Use the room/environment for conversation topic ideas:

"I was noticing the paintings on the walls in this room. Have you seen this one over here?"

Often, just the way you start the conversation creates a big shift. It breaks the ice and eases the awkwardness, leading to more natural conversation. From there, you can keep the engagement going.

As you talk, listen to hear what the other person cares about, what challenges they might be facing, or what excites them. This might be their pets, their kids, or some interesting industry trend. These nuggets are great for genuine rapport and relationship building.

Refill With Intention: Your CTA

Finally, move to a soft but intentional CTA. Close out the conversation with something like:

"This has been a great conversation. Can I grab your card? I'd love to connect in the near future."

"I read an interesting article on [topic you discussed] recently; mind if I send it your way?"

Your CTA should be subtle, not a hard push. Remember that business often happens after the event, fueled by the connections made during it. That's where your follow-up plan will come into play.

W: What About _______?—When Networking Feels Off-Track

Even with the best BREWing, networking can have its awkward or challenging moments. Here's how to handle a few common "blanks":

What if...you don't know anyone?

This is where your preset intention ("talk to three new people") becomes your lifeline. It gives you a mission. Take a deep breath, use your open posture and try one of those curious conversation starters.

What if...you're at a conference without a booth and feel adrift?

Again, focus back on the plan. Who did you research? Which sessions offer Q&A? What after-hours event can you target for specific connections? Having objectives prevents aimless wandering.

What if...everyone is in tight cliques?

Look for someone on the edge of a group or someone else standing alone. A simple, "Hi, mind if I join you for a moment? I'm Amy," can often work. If not, move on gracefully.

What if...the conversation lulls awkwardly?

Refer back to your surroundings. "This venue is impressive, isn't it?" Or, if you've built some rapport: "Aside from [work topic], what are you passionate about these days?" Or kindly move on. "I'd better go say hello to a few more people. It was great meeting you."

What if...you have to be there but just aren't feeling it?

We all have those days. Revert to a micro-goal from your 'B' prep: "Okay, my only job for the next 30 minutes is to genuinely engage with one new person and get their business card." Give yourself permission for it to be a small win.

Networking: A Continuous Brew

The most effective networking doesn't end when the lights go out at the venue. That's often just the beginning. By "Warming the Mug" with intentional prep and confident presence, "Stirring the Conversation" with genuine curiosity, aiming to "Refill with Intention" by securing a next step, and committing to keep pouring value into the relationship over time, you transform networking from a necessary evil into a powerful engine for building momentum.

Espresso Shot: Your Challenge

Before your next networking event, your challenge is to define and write down ONE specific, actionable, non-salesy goal for your attendance.

Examples:

- Learn one new industry trend from three different people.
- Identify one person who works at X company and have a conversation.
- Secure one coffee meeting follow-up.

Hold yourself accountable to this single intention.

Summary: BREW in Networking

B: Be the Moment

- Remember that your intention isn't to "get clients" on the spot. It's to make three new connections, learn something new, or secure one to two follow-up conversations.

- Have a plan. Ditch the "safety nets" (running to the bar, hiding behind your phone). Set your goals before you walk in the room.
- Prep your presence: Have your nonverbal cues primed—phone away, open posture, ready to make eye contact.

R: Raise Confidence

- Stick to the plan. Your structure is your biggest confidence booster and reduces the anxiety of "winging it."
- Project openness. Use confident posture and visible hands to appear approachable and invite connection, even when you don't feel 100% comfortable.
- Have the confidence to ask questions beyond the generic "What do you do?" and to break away from the safety of your usual group.

E: Engage

- Ditch default questions and stale conversation starters. Instead, spark conversations based on the environment ("That cocktail looks interesting." or "Is this your first time at this event?").
- Ask questions about what *they* care about to build a genuine relationship, not just to pass the time.
- End with a soft CTA. The goal is the next small step ("Mind if I send you that article?" or "Perhaps we could grab coffee next week?").

W: What About _______?

- *What if...you don't know anyone?* Revert to your preset goal of meeting three new people. Find someone on the edge of a group or standing alone and introduce yourself.
- *What if...the conversation lulls?* Comment on the surroundings to restart the flow.
- *What if...you're "not feeling it"?* Set a micro-goal: "I will talk to two new people, and then I can make a polite exit."

CHAPTER 12

Meetings—Stop Wasting Time, Start Brewing Momentum

Let's move on to our next step in the sales process: meetings. This is where connections are deepened, value is demonstrated, and momentum is built. Of course, as we all know, meetings don't always go that way.

In fact, a whopping 71% of meetings are considered unproductive and inefficient.[32] Yikes. Just because you're leading a meeting doesn't mean you're doing it well—yet.

> **A WHOPPING 71% OF MEETINGS ARE CONSIDERED UNPRODUCTIVE AND INEFFICIENT.**

32 Leslie A. Perlow, Constance Noonan Hadley, and Eunice Eun, "Stop the Meeting Madness: How to Free Up Time for Meaningful Work," *Harvard Business Review* 95, no. 4 (2017): 62-69, https://hbr.org/2017/07/stop-the-meeting-madness.

The good news is that you can break the mold and turn meetings into momentum machines. Here's how to apply the BREW Method to every meeting you lead:

B: Be the Moment in Meetings—Control Every Step

As we established in chapter 6, "Being the Moment" is all about having intention and structure. This is what creates credibility and shows clients that you are someone they can trust. First, let's talk intention, starting with *what you want your client to remember*. You have an hour's worth of information to give them. How much of it are they going to remember by the end of the day? According to The Forgetting Curve from chapter 3, 20% *at best*. If we're being honest about where we fall in our client's priority list, it's probably closer to 10%. They've got work and other meetings and family life and a whole laundry list of other shit occupying their mind.

Your job is to know the 10% you want them to remember and create moments to make that 10% stick.

How do you do that? Figure out your 10% and repeat it. Make sure you recap the most important information at the end of the meeting. Then, send a follow-up email with that information. Reinforce, repeat, and make sure the message gets remembered.

Structuring Your Meeting

In a meeting, structure means leading the conversation from the very first second. We're going to cover three easy-to-remember frameworks to help you structure a strong meeting from beginning to end.

The Opening

The goal of your opening is to gain your client's attention. You can't do that if you start your meeting the same way everyone else does.

Instead of the typical round-robin introductions, "Everyone say your name and title," try this: You concisely introduce yourself and your team members present, briefly stating their relevance. Then, turn it to the client: "I'm Amy, CEO of Sales & Presence, and I have Steve here who runs our operations and will be key in [relevant area]. We're thrilled to be here. I didn't know if you'd like to do formal introductions on your side or if you're ready to dive right in?"

You give them the option, toss out the typical ritual, and immediately signal a more dynamic approach. It's just enough of a change to make an impact.

Another piece of the opening where it's easy to lose momentum is the typical "About Us" slide. (Once again, boring and outdated.) Your company's mission, how many years you've been in business—that information is online, and your client has probably already read about it. What they want to know is *how you can help them.*

Instead of boring background info, focus on "Here's How We Help." This sets up the foundation early in the meeting that you are there to provide solutions and help the client reach their goals. (And if your company won't let you change the slide, then change your talking points; structure what you say in a way that focuses on how you help clients.)

ACT: The Meeting Opening Framework

Here's a framework called ACT to keep you on track and build in structure that creates credibility and trust:

A: First, you **Appreciate**—start with a simple, genuine appreciation for their time.

"Good morning, everyone. Thanks so much for making the time to connect today," sets a positive, respectful tone right away.

C: Next, you **Confirm** the time available.

"It looks like we have an hour scheduled. Does that timeframe still work for everyone?"

This simple question gives you control. If someone needs to leave early, you know upfront and can manage it professionally, preventing awkward disruptions later and showing respect for everyone's schedule.

T: Finally, and most importantly, **Together, set the goal.** Remember that your meeting is about the client; your agenda is simply the roadmap you've prepared to help *them* achieve *their* goal for this interaction.

"The goal today is to learn more about what's top-of-mind for you in your business and see where we can offer support. And the way we're going to do that is [three points from your agenda]."

Using the ACT framework immediately signals that this meeting will be different—respectful, collaborative, and *focused on them.*

Structuring the Middle

Now that you have the opening of the meeting locked in, it's time to gather information. How? By talking less about yourself and your product and asking more questions instead—more specifically, asking the right questions the right way. Let's talk about how to format your questions effectively.

GUIDE: The Framework for Discovering More

G: Gather Context

Ask some basic fact-finding questions that help settle everyone in. Remember this doesn't mean asking questions you already know the answer to. A quick 1% shift is to reframe known information as a statement, then ask a deeper question you don't know the answer to.

For example, instead of, "So, how long has your company been in business?" Try: "I saw on LinkedIn that your agency just celebrated its 10-year anniversary, which is a huge accomplishment. In those 10 years, what has been the biggest operational success you've had as the team has scaled?"

U: Understand Needs (The Pain Point)

Understand your client's needs by asking about pain points. Most salespeople are pretty good at doing this; just make sure you're digging deeper by asking questions.

For example, if you ask your client what challenges they're facing and they say something like, "Thanks! Honestly, it's managing project workflows. When we were smaller, it was easy. Now, with more clients and remote team members, things are constantly falling through the cracks."

You can probe deeper with, "That's a common growing pain. When you say things are 'falling through the cracks,' what does that typically look like for your team?"

The real magic, however, happens in the next step.

I: Identify the Impact

Asking questions is important but only if you're listening to hear, not listening to respond. Most of the time we ask a question, get an answer, and then jump right to our product or solution. Don't do this. You need to keep asking questions until you get to the real, tangible impact those pain points are having for your client.

Brew It Better	
Instead of this…	Try this…
Jumping straight to your solution:	Digging deeper to uncover the impact:

<table>
<tr><td>

Client: "Our biggest challenge is usually missed deadlines. A designer finishes their part, but the copywriter doesn't get notified, so the project just sits there for a couple of days until someone realizes it's stalled. It's really frustrating."

You: "We see this a lot. Our software helps you seamlessly run your workflow so everything keeps moving right away. Here's how…"

</td><td>

Client: "Our biggest challenge is usually missed deadlines. A designer finishes their part, but the copywriter doesn't get notified, so the project just sits there for a couple of days until someone realizes it's stalled. It's really frustrating."

You: "I can see how that would be frustrating. What's the impact of those two-day stalls on your client relationships or the team's overall capacity?"

</td></tr>
</table>

Which of these shows that you actually care about your client? In the first example, you jump right into you, you, you. Even if what you're saying is true, it doesn't feel authentic. Why? It misses the big impact—the *real* reason why this is a problem for the client.

The second example, on the other hand, leads you to the deeper "why" and gives you the opportunity to offer better, more meaningful solutions. That's what builds trust. That's what shows credibility.

D: Demonstrate Understanding

Summarize what they've said back to them in their own words to show that you've listened and are working to understand what they need.

Client: "That's the real problem. It's not just a delay; it means we might miss a client's campaign launch date, which makes us look unreliable and puts that account renewal at risk. Plus, the last-minute scrambles to fix these things are causing serious burnout."

You: "Okay, so to make sure I'm tracking, the issue isn't just about internal workflows. It's that these communication gaps are leading to missed deadlines, which in turn puts important client renewals at risk and is causing burnout on your team. Do I have that right?"

E: Empathetic Solution

Finally, wrap it up into an empathetic solution that focuses on your client and their needs. This is where it's easy to jump into the pitch or focus on your product. Resist that temptation.

"That sounds incredibly stressful to manage, especially when you're trying to grow. It seems like the core challenge is creating that clear visibility so the team isn't working in silos. Understanding that, I'm wondering if it would be helpful to explore a system designed to automatically move projects from one stage to the next, to help reduce that burnout and protect those crucial client relationships."

This is how you keep the momentum moving forward, build credibility, and really connect with your client.

Structuring the Close

Let's pretend you just ran the most badass meeting ever. Then, at the end, you smile, thank the client, tell them you'll email a follow-up, and walk away, sure that they are absolutely going to want to work with you.

What happens next? If that's how you ended your meeting, *nothing does*. This isn't a close—it's a missed opportunity. You've left things open ended, confusing, and with no direction. You can't assume a client knows what the next step is, and you can't leave it to them to follow up with you to ask.

Don't make the mistake of running the ball down the field only to fumble at the one-yard line. You have to structure your close and your CTA.

The goal of a powerful close is to lead to the next step and give your client confidence in you to take that next step. That happens when you lay out exactly what is coming next for you and for them.

The REPS Framework for Closing

R: Start with a concise **Recap** of what you covered.

"I see we have about five minutes left, so I want to be mindful of your time and make sure we wrap up with a clear plan. To quickly recap, it sounds like the main challenge with your current workflow is that communication gaps are leading to project stalls, which is ultimately putting client renewals at risk and causing team burnout."

E: From there, you **Explore** any lingering questions or topics that were missed, ensuring everyone feels heard. Go beyond "any questions" (a phrase that almost guarantees everyone will tune you out and nobody will actually ask you anything).

"Great. Before we talk about next steps, I want to explore if there was anything we discussed that's still unclear or anything important we might have missed from your perspective?"

P: Most importantly, you establish the **Plan of Action.** This is your "confidence to act" moment where you explicitly state your next steps with a timeline, then clearly state their expected next steps, also with a proposed timeline, and get their agreement.

You: "Here's the plan of action then. I'm going to prepare a brief, customized demo video that shows you exactly how our system handles that handoff between your designers and copywriters. I will have that in your inbox by end of day Friday.

From your side, to make that demo as relevant as possible, could you send me a simple list of the key stages in your current project workflow? How does getting that to me by the end of day tomorrow sound?"

Client: "Yes, I can do that"

You: "Excellent. If things get busy and I don't see it come through, I'll send a quick reminder the day after tomorrow."

S: Finally, if the timing is right and there's a clear opening, you **Set the Next Meeting** right then and there.

"Fantastic. Once you've had a chance to review that demo, our next logical step would be a 30-minute call to discuss it and answer any questions. How about we tentatively set that meeting now for next Thursday, September 4th, at 2:00 p.m. CDT? I can send an invite, and we can always adjust if needed."

How would *you* feel if someone ended a meeting with you that way? Would you trust them? Yep. There's no ambiguity. There's nothing vague. This is real leadership, real structure—you are the conductor making sure everything moves forward.

Brew It Better	
Instead of this…	Try this…
Ineffective Close	Structured BREW Close
"Well, we're out of time for today. I'll send an email to recap everything. Thanks!" (Vague, leaving them unsure of what to do next or when they're going to hear from you.)	"I know we're about five minutes from the top of the hour, so I want to be mindful of your time and make sure we wrap up clearly. From our side, the next step is that we're going to send you the proposal we discussed, including the pricing and those few additions you were interested in. You'll have that from us by end of day today. I know we talked about you getting us a list of those targeted areas in the states you really want to focus on. How does tomorrow by end of day sound for you to get that over to us?" (Wait for their confirmation or suggest an alternative if needed). "Great. If I don't hear back from you by tomorrow end of day with that list, I'll plan to follow up with you on Monday morning around 9 a.m., just to see if you have any further questions or if we can support you in getting that information together."

See the difference? With a strong structured close, you're setting expectations. You're driving the next step. You're putting time parameters on everything (this is a MUST). You're keeping the momentum going. And you're leading the entire process forward

R: Raise Confidence in Meetings (for Yourself and Others)

One of the best ways to raise your confidence in a meeting is to stay anchored in your structure—when in doubt, remind yourself of the frameworks in this chapter and where you planned to take the conversation. When you lead with structure, you not only give yourself confidence, but you also convey credibility. That's what gives others the confidence to want to work with you.

And, if your structure is your engine, then your nonverbal communication is your transmission, putting your confidence into motion and projecting it so you can solidify your leadership in the room.

This comes back to everything we unpacked in chapter 7—your ornaments, your posture, your hands, your eye contact. These pieces are vital in a meeting.

To recap: First, dress for the atmosphere of the meeting. Choose your colors based on what you want to project. Dress in tailored, professional clothing. And find ways to let your personality shine through.

The meeting starts before the meeting: Think about how you walk into the building, the elevator, and the meeting room.

Think about how you physically occupy your space at the table. Are you leaning back with your arms crossed, or are you leaning forward slightly, signaling engagement and interest? An open posture (arms uncrossed, body angled toward the speaker) invites collaboration.

Keep your hands visible, not hidden under the table, stuffed in your pockets, or anxiously clasped in your lap. It's a simple but powerful nonverbal signal that says, "I'm open, I'm transparent, I have nothing to hide."

Finally, use your eye contact to command the room. As you speak, make a point to connect with *everyone* at the table, not just the person with the most senior title. A brief, direct glance to each person as you make a point makes them feel included and valued and reinforces your role as the leader of the conversation.

When these pieces accompany a strong structure, they create a feedback loop: Your structure builds confidence, your self-assured nonverbal cues project that confidence, and that projection in turn reinforces your own feeling of control.

E: Engage in Meetings—Guiding the Conversation for Impact

The frameworks in this chapter, like the GUIDE framework for the middle of a meeting, give valuable structure. Engagement is the art of bringing that conversational structure to life through how you listen and how you speak.

The GUIDE framework is impossible without real listening. As we covered in chapter 8, this means shifting from "listening to respond" to "listening to understand."

As you ask questions and dive deeper into your client's pain points, remember to stay curious, stay in the moment, and practice the power of the pause and waiting to take in what your client is truly saying before you respond.

Try to listen to what is going on beneath the surface, really identifying that deeper impact. This gives you a window to offer so much more value.

The truth is that people live with pain points all the time; we all do. And we're usually willing to live with them until their impact is greater than the hassle of change.

I once had an annoying security system that was always beeping, alerting me about a low battery. And over and over again, I just overrode the system. But what if there had been a break-in? That impact would have been enough to trigger an action.

It's your job to help the client see the full, often unacknowledged, impact of their current pain and offer solutions without just focusing on your pitch.

For example, don't just hear "our current system is slow" and jump to your solution "our system is five times faster." Engage deeper. Ask, "When that system is slow, what's the impact on your team's productivity or your client deliverables?" Helping your client articulate the *real-world consequences* of their pain is what creates the urgency and desire for change.

Finally, remember that when you're engaging, you need to be in the moment. Don't miss the chance for connection points. If your client mentions a love of baseball, that's a potential connection point. They say something about a child? Maybe you have kids and a great story to share. Do you notice a regional accent? There's a chance for some personal questions.

The bottom line is that engagement isn't scripted. You stick to your overall structure, but remember that you're making moments, forming connections, and building relationships—and those all require being in the moment and actually communicating like a human being.

W: What About _______?–When Meetings Go Off-Script

No matter how well you structure your meeting with ACT, GUIDE, and REPS, things can still go sideways. People get distracted, agendas get hijacked, and tech fails. Here's how to handle those moments:

What if...someone hijacks the agenda with an off-topic issue?

Remember—you control the meeting, and it's your job to make sure that everyone's time is used wisely. Acknowledge the point's importance, and gently guide the conversation back to stay on track. Try this: "That's a really important point, David. Thank you for bringing that up. I know we have roughly 45 minutes left, so I'd like to continue that discussion offline, as I know we still need to cover X today."

(And of course, sometimes meetings will flow in and out of direction. That doesn't make them unsuccessful—you just need to be the leader who keeps the momentum going.)

What if...you get a tough question you can't answer on the spot?

Don't bluff. Own it. "That's an excellent question. Let me circle back with my team, and I'll get back with you on it by the end of the day." Confidence isn't knowing everything. It's knowing how to follow through.

What if...someone is completely disengaged (on their phone, looking out the window)?

Don't call them out. Sometimes, it doesn't matter if someone is disengaged, especially in a bigger group. If it's important, gently re-engage them with a direct but respectful question. "Sarah, I'd be particularly interested in your perspective on this, given your experience with..." This invites them back into the conversation without creating conflict.

The bottom line to remember is that you are driving the action. Stick to your structure and your intention, without missing moments to engage. This helps you navigate the what-ifs and get back on track.

Espresso Shot: Your Challenge

End your next meeting strong. Explicitly state your next action *with a timeline,* along with *their next action with a proposed timeline,* and get their agreement.

Summary: BREW in Meetings

B: Be the Moment

- The ACT opening: Structure your opening to grab attention.
  - » Appreciate their time
  - » Confirm the timeframe
  - » Together, set the goal (focused on *their* desired outcome)
- The GUIDE conversation framework: Structure the middle of the meeting to guide the discovery process from context and pain to business impact and solutions.
  - » Gather context with fact-finding questions (ones you *don't* already know the answer to).
  - » Understand needs. Uncover the pain point, and keep asking questions.
  - » Identify the impact. Don't jump to your solution. Keep digging to find out why the pain point really matters.
  - » Demonstrate understanding. Repeat what they said back to them, using their words.
  - » Offer empathetic solutions. Resist the temptation to skip to the pitch.
- The REPS closing framework: Structure your close for clear momentum.
  - » Recap key points.
  - » Explore any missed items.
  - » Outline the plan of action (your steps + timeline, their steps + timeline).
  - » Set the next meeting.

R: Raise Confidence

- Use confidence from Control: Your structural frameworks (ACT, GUIDE, REPS) eliminate uncertainty and boost your confidence as the meeting leader.
- Focus on your nonverbal cues: Use confident meeting posture (leaning in slightly), keep hands visible on the table, and make eye contact with everyone in the room to project leadership.

E: Engage

- Listen to understand, not to respond: Practice the "power of the pause" after someone speaks to truly hear them, not just to plan your own response.
- Ask impact questions: Don't just stop at identifying a pain point. Engage them on its business consequences: "What is the tangible *impact* of that on your team?"
- Speak with empathy: When offering a solution, first acknowledge their feeling or the impact of their problem ("Wow, it sounds like that issue is causing a lot of stress...").

W: What About _______?

- *What if...someone hijacks the agenda?* Acknowledge their point, suggest a separate discussion ("park it"), and gently guide the conversation back to the agreed-upon goal.
- *What if...you're asked a question you can't answer?* Don't bluff. Confidently state you will find the correct information and follow up by a specific, promised time.
- *What if...someone is disengaged?* Avoid calling them out. If necessary, gently re-engage them with a direct question that values their expertise ("Sarah, I'd be interested in your perspective on this...").

CHAPTER 13

Presentation—Creating Moments That Command the Room

Presentations are high-stakes. Whether you're in a boardroom with five executives or on a stage in front of 500 people, this is a moment where all eyes are on you. That also means that it's an opportunity for credibility and momentum.

Why do so many sales presentations fall completely flat? They follow the same, tired, typical formula. They're boring. They're predictable. They're a data dump, not a dynamic experience.

The presenter (you) often gets lazy, lets the slides lead them, and closes with a weak "Any questions?" leaving the room with a fizzle instead of a bang.

If that sounds familiar, it's no fault of your own. That's how you were taught to do it. You weren't taught to create engagement—you were taught to pitch the product.

Let's reframe it. We're focusing on creating memorable moments that resonate with your audience.

Here's how:

B: Be the Moment in Presentations—Your Blueprint for Impact

To "Be the Moment," you need an intentional blueprint for your presentation. Setting your structure and your intention will help you overcome your nerves and keep you focused on what you're presenting and how you're communicating it.

As always, start with your intention. Before you build a single slide, define your objective. What is the one thing you want your audience to think, feel, or do after you've finished speaking? Is it to feel confident in a new strategy? To be curious about your solution? To agree to a next step? Whatever your intention, it's going to pave the way for the overall story that your presentation tells. For a presentation, everything needs to be built around your through line, meaning the single core idea or word that connects all of your points.

For example, the through line for this book is *connection*. Moments create connection. The BREW Method creates connection. Connection is what sets you apart in the sales world.

Your through line will thread together through a cohesive narrative. It might be *simplicity*, *partnership*, or *growth*. This theme becomes your anchor, the recurring concept you weave throughout to make your message powerful and memorable.

This can also help you determine what you should say and *not say*. When in doubt, return to your through line. If a point or a story isn't connected to it, consider whether it belongs or needs to be tossed out.

Structure Your Content Flow

With your intention and through line set, you can structure the key parts of your presentation.

The Impactful Open

Just like with a meeting, you only have a few seconds in a presentation to capture your audience's intention. Ditch the boring "Hi, my name is Amy, and today we're going to talk about..."

Instead, plan an immediate engagement. Your structure might include starting with a compelling question, a surprising statistic, a "show of hands" prompt, or having everyone write down one thing they hope to learn. 79% of people prefer interactive presentations that give them a chance to participate.[33] Why? It's less boring and more memorable.

It's easy for people to zone out and not pay attention to what you're saying. When you create engagement, it pulls your audience into the moment and encourages them to participate, make connections, and actually listen to you.

---

33 Aayush Jain, "Top Presentation Insights & Statistics [2024]," *INK PPT Blog*, June 24, 2024, https://www.inkppt.com/post/top-presentation-insights-statistics-2024.

The Strong Middle

The #1 rule for a strong presentation is *don't let your slides lead you*. Meaning, don't pause and wait for the next slide, then jump into reading from it. Instead, you need to be the leader of your slides. You can create verbal transitions that connect ideas between slides and take away the passive, boring feeling that often happens in slide-by-slide presentations.

A powerful transition often poses a question that the next slide answers. "So we've covered the challenge with the current market. What does that really mean for the state of your industry? [Click to next slide]" This creates flow and proves you're in command, not just getting lazy and reading headlines that your audience can read for themselves. You're leading the slides.

The Powerful Close

How you end your presentation matters. Don't just let it trail off. Structure your ending with a concise recap of your key takeaways, brought together one last time by your powerful through line. Know your final words and deliver them with conviction before closing with a simple, confident "Thank you."

R: Raise Confidence for Presentations—Owning Your Nerves and the Stage

By now you understand that a solid structure is your single greatest confidence and credibility booster. When you know your story, your flow, and your key messages, you can stop worrying about what to say and focus on how you deliver it.

But even with the best plan, the internal jitters have a way of kicking in.

That is one reason that raising confidence is about managing your nerves and owning the room with your physical presence. Here are four key strategies for embodying and projecting confidence when presenting:

Anchor Yourself in Who You Are

When nerves spike, we tend to forget our abilities and expertise and, most importantly, our own worth. Before you present, ground yourself by recalling three to five core truths about yourself that have nothing to do with work—things no one can take away. (Mine are: I'm crazy for dogs and cats, I can't live without coffee, and I love running with the sun on my face.) These anchors remind you that no matter what happens, you are still who you are. Nothing in the presentation can change that. This can take away your nerves and ground you as you prepare to step onstage.

Leverage Eye Contact (The Rule of Three)

A room full of faces can be overwhelming. Don't try to connect with everyone. Instead, shrink the room by planning to focus on just three friendly faces in different sections. This turns a daunting performance into a series of focused, one-on-one connections.

If you lock eyes with someone who's looking down at their phone, don't let it throw you; simply move on to one of your other chosen points of focus. You'll never win 100% of the room, so give your energy to those who are leaning in.

Plan Your Movement

Movement can be helpful in a presentation, but without structure it's easy to fidget or wander aimlessly. These things can weaken your presence.

> YOU'LL NEVER WIN 100% OF THE ROOM, SO GIVE YOUR ENERGY TO THOSE WHO ARE LEANING IN.

Instead, think about when and why you want to move. Maybe you're on stage and you want to intentionally move to the left, right, and middle. Or maybe you're in the front of the room and you intentionally walk around to the side of a table on a certain point. Structure your movement around key points in your presentation to create impact around moments you want your audience to remember.

My favorite way to bring in movement is to start a presentation at the back or side of the room and then walk up to the front or stage. It gets the attendees engaged and helps me with my confidence.

There's no one "right" way to move. The key is in the structure and the practice. Don't assume that your movements will come naturally. Plan them, practice them, and get intentional.

Use Your Breath as a Tool

This is a simple but powerful physiological hack. (Those of you who are yogis and meditation peeps already know this.) Just before you begin speaking, take one slow, deep breath in. Then, start talking on the exhale. This does two things: It calms your sympathetic nervous system, physically reducing the feeling of anxiety, and it helps keep your vocal pitch from rising, allowing you to start with a calm, controlled tone.

Power Pose

Remember the science from chapter 7: Your body tells your brain how to feel. And in a presentation, you want your body to tell your brain to feel confident. There's no better way to do that than a quick Power Pose.

Before you step onstage, find a private space such as the hallway or the restroom. Then stand in your big, widespread power pose, with your hands on your hips. Do this for two minutes—it has been scientifically proven to boost your confidence.

Own the Space

You raise confidence by owning the stage physically. Your posture, as we've discussed, sends powerful signals to your own brain. Stand tall, keep your shoulders back, and use open gestures. If you really want to project confidence and command attention from the start, try this technique: Don't start on the stage. Begin speaking from the back or side of the room and walk purposefully to the front as you deliver your opening lines. It's an immediate pattern interruption that signals you're in complete control.

Two Hours to Panel: Confidence in Action

After I spoke at a recent training, a young woman approached me, clearly stressed, wanting to know how to appear more confident.

"How do you do that?" she asked. "I have to sit on a panel to talk about our work, and I know I'll be asked questions. I'm terrified of speaking to large groups. How do I handle it?"

My first thought was to schedule a coaching call, but then I asked, "When is this panel?"

"In two hours."

Two hours! Okay, deep coaching was out. She needed emergency prep. I gave her three immediate actions:

1. Presence: I taught her how to Power Pose and encouraged her to take a few minutes before the panel to position her body for confidence. I also encouraged her to sit straight up on the panel to project that confidence in the room.
2. Focus: "You're overwhelmed because you're thinking about the whole room," I told her. "Scan the audience and pick three friendly faces in different sections. Focus on talking directly to them and maintaining eye contact as you answer questions."
3. Remember who you are: I told her to forget the panel for a second, take a deep breath, and think of three things that made her uniquely her.

She emailed me the next day gushing about her experience. She put those three steps into action, crushed it at the panel, and showed up with confidence, power, and ownership (and she received several compliments as a result).

E: Engage in Presentations—Creating a Shared Experience

With your structure planned and your confidence high, the actual presentation becomes about engagement. Again, engagement in a presentation looks different: After all, if you're the only one talking, that inherently means that your audience is sitting still, expected to listen.

It's an entirely different dynamic than a meeting. But the core philosophy is the same; you need your audience to be invested and feel that they are getting real value.

We've all sat in presentations where after a bit of time, we tuned out. So how do you avoid your audience pressing the mental mute button? By creating a shared experience instead of just delivering information.

This starts with reading the energy in the room. If you come in rushing full of energy and excitement and the audience is the opposite, you're missing the mark. You want to be authentic, and you want to create engagement, but you need to consider who you're speaking to and how to draw them in.

If you're in a boardroom, try a simple name callout. "Sam, would love to hear your thoughts on this before we head into the meeting."

In virtual presentations or meetings, ask people to respond in chat or raise virtual hands. We have tools to help encourage engagement virtually—and far too often, we don't use them.

If it's a bigger in person presentation, find a way to get the audience involved. When you move, your brain gets stimulated, making it easier to learn and remember information.[34] That can be as simple as asking for a show of hands or having the audience write something down.

---

34 Raed Mualem et al., "The Effect of Movement on Cognitive Performance," *Frontiers in Public Health* 6 (2018): 100, https://doi.org/10.3389/fpubh.2018.00100.

You can also create engagement by telling a relatable story, incorporating humor, or asking the audience questions. You want people thinking, active, and invested.

W: What About ________?—Handling Presentation Mishaps

No matter how well you prepare, things can still go wrong. Here's how you handle the unexpected without derailing your presentation:

What if...the technology fails? It happens. Acknowledge it with grace and a bit of humor ("Well, it seems the tech gods have other plans for us!"). Because you've prepared your through line and key messages, and not just your slides, you are ready to speak without them if necessary—which also gives you the confidence to own the presentation, no matter what happens.

What if...you see someone disengaged or on their phone? You will never have 100% of the room. Accept it, and remember their disengagement isn't because of you. People have a million things going on in their brains and their lives—it's likely not about you. Move your eyes from the person looking at their phone and focus your energy on the friendly faces who are leaning in. Give your attention to the engaged, not the distracted.

What if...you lose your place? Your through line is your safety net. If you get lost, you can always pause, take a breath, and bring it back to your core theme to get back on track. For example: "Ultimately, what this all comes back to is [your through line]..."

What if...you do something awkward or embarrassing? It happens. Use it. I once stepped onstage to give a presentation and noticed a seam between two platforms in front of me. I realized right away that my high heels could easily get stuck in the gap, so I told myself, "Okay, whatever you do, avoid that spot." And what happened? Naturally, I walked right into it. My heel got caught, and I almost fell, with 500 people staring at me.

I could have clammed up and let it get to me or just continued with the presentation and pretended nothing happened. Instead, I decided to use it. I announced, "Did you all see that? Were you witness to that? You're welcome." It was funny. It actually created some engagement and something to remember. And it was relatable—who hasn't taken an awkward fall at some point?

It's All About Connection

Ultimately, a great presentation isn't about perfection or poise. Your objective is to build a bridge between you and your audience.

When you prep your content, structure intention, build your confidence, and find a creative way to engage your audience, that's exactly what you do; you connect, you stand out, and you leave a lasting impact.

Espresso Shot: Your Challenge

The "First Minute" Engagement Plan: For your very next presentation (even a small team update), your challenge is to plan one specific engagement tactic (a question, a show of hands, a "write this down" prompt) and execute it within the first 60 seconds.

Summary: BREW in Presentations

B: Be the Moment

- Find your through line. Identify a single word or theme (e.g., *connection, simplicity*) that connects all your points and weave it throughout.
- Plan an engagement tactic for the first 60 seconds (question, poll, show of hands).
- Plan your transitions. Know how you'll bridge from one slide to the next without just reading the title.
- Structure your close to be a concise recap built around your through line.

R: Raise Confidence

- Ground yourself with anchors. Before you start, remind yourself of three to five core, non-work truths about yourself to anchor your confidence in your inherent worth.
- Remember the rule of three for eye contact. Don't scan the crowd. Plan to make genuine eye contact with just three friendly faces in different parts of the room.
- Own the stage physically. Use open, confident posture. For an advanced move, start offstage and walk through the audience as you begin.

E: Engage

- Lead the slides; don't let them lead you.

- Incorporate movement or activity where you can (even virtually).
- Adjust your energy and pacing based on the audience's real-time feedback.

W: What About _______?

- *What if...the tech fails?* Acknowledge it with grace. Be prepared enough with your core message to continue without slides if necessary.
- *What if...someone is disengaged?* Ignore them. Focus your energy and eye contact on the people who *are* leaning in.

CHAPTER 14

Following Up—The Art of Building Momentum

After you've prospected, networked, or brewed connection in a meeting, what happens next? For far too many of us, the answer is…*nothing*. Crickets. Being ghosted.

The truth is that even great salespeople often struggle with follow up. And that's unfortunate, because statistically, it often takes at least five touchpoints to get a "yes," but a staggering 44% of salespeople give up after just one attempt.[35] They send one email, hear silence, and walk away because they're afraid to bother people or they don't know what to say.

My take on that statistic? This isn't bad news. It's *the biggest opportunity you have*. While nearly half of your competition is dropping out of the race after the first lap, you have a wide-open field to make an impact. Game on.

---

35 Lisa Ross, "The Importance of Sale Follow-Ups – Statistics." Invesp, June 8, 2023, https://www.invespcro.com/blog/sale-follow-ups/.

So, let's break down how to apply the BREW Method to your follow-up, so you can keep your momentum going strong.

B: Be the Moment in Follow-Up—Your Cadence & Intention

If follow-up feels awkward for you, you're not alone. Let's think about it differently. Instead of viewing follow-up as another task you "have to do," think of it as a trust builder.

> **INSTEAD OF VIEWING FOLLOW-UP AS ANOTHER TASK YOU "HAVE TO DO," THINK OF IT AS A TRUST BUILDER.**

You've already piqued interest or formed a connection with someone. Your intention is to continue building trust, and structure is how you do that.

Follow-up structure falls into two main buckets:

1. The "New Connection" Follow-Up Cadence: This is for someone you've just met (at that Super Bowl party, a conference, or after a first meeting). Your intention in this case is to solidify the connection and move to the next step *quickly*. The biggest mistake salespeople make here is waiting too long because they don't want to "bother" them. And what happens? You lose momentum. You miss the opportunity to take advantage of the initial connection. And you send the signal that you're not really interested.

   What do you do instead? Let's say you met someone at an event Friday. Don't wait two weeks. Call them *Monday* with a brief, relevant follow-up. Then immediately send an email referencing that call. Just like in your cold outreach from chapter 10, you've established multiple touchpoints in the first day.

Then, on Wednesday, go ahead and connect on LinkedIn. Thursday, call again. You're creating multiple early touchpoints to show you're serious and engaged.

2. The "Existing Client/Long-Term Nurture" Cadence: For clients you're already working with or prospects who are on a longer timeline, the structure is different. This is about staying top-of-mind by consistently providing value.

   The cadence is slower—maybe monthly or quarterly, reaching out with valuable, non-salesy touchpoints like a relevant newsletter, a link to a podcast you know they'd like, or an article about their industry.

   Remember that in both buckets of follow-up, your intention is never just to "check in." Your intention is always to add value: Show you were listening by referencing what's valuable *to them*.

R: Raise Confidence in Follow-Up—It's Not Pushy

It's easy to feel confident right after a great meeting when the energy is high. The real test of confidence comes a week later when you've sent a follow-up and been met with...silence.

This is where self-doubt creeps in. Your brain starts spinning stories: *Did I misread the room? Was I annoying? Did I completely blow it?* You start taking their silence personally and assuming that they aren't interested. You hesitate to send another email because you don't want to seem pushy or desperate.

The secret is to learn to detach your professional process from your personal feelings and let go of that self-doubt.

One way to do this is to center yourself on the value you're offering. If you've created an intention of value and you've moved beyond pushy pitches, you're not going to be bothering anyone. Step into the confidence that you are offering something valuable and that you truly want to help your prospects solve their problems.

Remember that following up isn't an empty "check-in." It's a professional continuation of a valuable conversation they participated in. You've already earned the right to be in their inbox.

Finally, remind yourself that when silence happens, it's almost never about you. It's about their overflowing inbox, their competing priorities, their own internal meetings they need to have before getting back to you. Confidence is the ability to depersonalize their silence and understand it as simply a reflection of their busy world. You're not bothering them; you're professionally persisting through their noise.

When you find that a prospect isn't returning calls or emails, step back and depersonalize the situation. Did you miss a red flag in your last meeting (like a pending merger or a timeline that wasn't urgent)? This can give you a path forward and a plan of action for how to approach your next touchpoint.

This mindset is what empowers you to send a bold, direct subject line and use a strong CTA. You're not being pushy; you're being a clear, professional partner who is taking the lead to move a mutually beneficial conversation forward.

E: Engage in Follow-Up—The Art of the Re-Engagement

Now let's talk about how you engage in your follow-up. It's time to banish the weak, generic, typical follow-up phrases from your vocabulary forever.

DITCH THESE IMMEDIATELY:

- "Just checking in..."
- "Following up on our conversation..."
- "Circling back..."

These phrases scream, "I have nothing of value to add, but I'm supposed to email you."

Instead, your engagement must be direct, personal, and value-driven. Reference specific things you and your prospect discussed before. Always add value. And stick with strong, impactful language and you-framing.

Here's an example of what this looks like, in the form of a re-engagement email when a client hasn't reached back out:

Subject Line: Wednesday, May 10th.

This is just like the strategy from prospecting emails, but in reverse—reference the last meeting you had. It triggers their brain to ask, "What about that meeting did I forget?" creating an urgent need to open it.

Email Body:

Start with a human touch: "Hope all is well with you on this Thursday before the long weekend."

Reference *their* words and impact: "When we last connected, we were discussing your move to a new vendor to improve turnaround time efficiency. I recall these points being top-of-mind for you that day:" (Then use bullet points to list three key impacts/pains *they* mentioned).

End with a strong close to create the confidence to act: "I'd like to continue that conversation. How does next Wednesday at 1:00 p.m. look for a quick 15-minute call to discuss next steps?" Giving the other person a specific day and time makes it an easy yes.

Brew It Better	
Instead of this…	Try this…
Hi Sarah, I'm just circling back on our conversation from last week. I thought it was a great discussion and wanted to see if you had any questions about our platform. Let me know what your thoughts are when you have a moment. Best, Amy	Hi Sarah, Hope your week is off to a great start. When we connected a couple of weeks ago, we discussed the challenges of scaling your social media efforts. I recall these points being top-of-mind for you: • Maintaining brand consistency across all channels without adding more work for your team • Reducing the time spent creating content from scratch for each platform • Getting clear data to actually prove the ROI of your social strategy I'd like to continue that conversation. How does next Tuesday, October 21st, at 2:00 p.m. CDT look for a quick 15-minute call to discuss the next steps? Looking forward to connecting, Amy

The first email screams "checking a box." It's weak, generic, adds no value, and puts all the work on the client to restart the conversation. In other words, it's an email that is very easy to ignore.

The reframe is structured, confident, and immediately brings the client back to the value and impact they discussed. It respects their time by being direct and makes it easy for them to take the next step.

W: What About _______?—When Your Follow-Up Hits a Wall

What if...they still don't respond after your re-engagement attempts?

You have your answer. It is a "no, not now." Move them from your active follow-up cadence to your long-term (quarterly) nurture cadence. The pressure is off; you'll now focus on providing occasional, no-strings-attached value.

What if...they respond with "Now's not a good time"? Perfect! This is information, not rejection. Respond with respect and maintain control of the future. "Completely understand, thanks for letting me know. To respect your time, I'll plan to connect with you around the start of next quarter to see if the timing is better then. All the best until then." You've honored their request while professionally structuring a future touchpoint.

Espresso Shot: Your Challenge

Scroll through your "sent" emails to prospects. What are your go-to subject lines for follow-ups? Are they generic and boring?

For your next follow-up email, try the time-based subject line tactic ("Wednesday, May 10th") and see what kind of response it gets.

Summary: BREW in Follow-Up

B: Be the Moment

- Reframe your intention. You're there to add value and move the conversation forward to a clear next step.
- Use two different types of cadences:
  - » New connections: a fast, condensed sequence of touchpoints (call, email, social) within the first week to maintain momentum.
  - » Existing clients/nurture: a slower (monthly/quarterly) cadence focused on providing consistent, non-salesy value.
- Investigate before re-engaging: If a prospect has gone silent ("ghosted"), figure out what you might have missed in previous interactions before reaching out.

R: Raise Confidence

- Center yourself on the value you're offering.
- Let go of self-doubt and have the confidence to execute your planned sequence without second-guessing every step.
- Depersonalize silence. Reframe their silence as being about *their* priorities, not a personal rejection of you. This detaches your ego and prevents desperation.

E: Engage

- Ban "just checking in" and "following up on" from your vocabulary.
- When re-engaging a silent prospect, lead with a human touch, reference *their* specific pain points from your last conversation, and propose a clear CTA
- Use curiosity-driven subject lines: Apply the principle of using time/dates (e.g., "Wednesday, May 10th") to create FOMO and get your email opened.
- Stick to value. For nurture follow-ups, send articles, podcasts, or insights related to *their* interests, not just your product features.

W: What About _______?

- *What if...they still don't respond after your re-engagement attempts?* Respect their silence. This is a clear "no, not now." Gracefully transition them to your long-term, low-touch nurture list. The active pursuit is over for now.
- *What if...they reply with "Now's not a good time"?* Maintain control by proposing a future check-in. "Completely understand. I'll plan to circle back around the start of next quarter. All the best until then."

CHAPTER 15

Negotiation— Conversations That Drive Performance

Now, let's talk negotiating. The word itself can feel heavy. It brings to mind a high-stakes battle where there's a winner and a loser.

This winner versus loser idea starts early. As kids, our first negotiating tactics were raw emotion—we cried, we hit, we threw tantrums when we didn't get our way. And what were we often told? "Play nice." "You need to share." "Don't cry."

But we weren't taught *how* to effectively communicate our needs or find a middle ground. For women especially, the message was often to sit down and be quiet. When we get into a professional negotiation or hard conversation, those old patterns come bubbling up and we feel uncomfortable.

And even though this is a problem for so many people, nobody's telling us how to fix it. I've been through my share of negotiation trainings, and frankly, many of them miss the mark. Why? They either make it more complicated than it needs to be or they teach aggressive tactics that feel inauthentic.

Negotiating doesn't need to be a battlefield approach where you come in ready to conquer. Negotiating is something that happens all day, every day.

Say it's Taco Tuesday, but you're craving Italian, and you want to convince your partner to eat where you want. You negotiate for pasta. Or your kid wants to wear rain boots on a sunny day and you have to decide whether to pick that battle or give in. Practically every interaction with another person is a negotiation.

The only difference in a sales context is the level of emotion and the stakes involved. If you can remove the emotion and reframe the stakes, you can change your approach and your outcome.

B: Be the Moment in Negotiating—Setting Up Structure for the Win-Win

Just like in the other phases of the sales process, you cannot "wing" a negotiation. You need to go in with intention and have a plan for how to move through the conversation productively.

Let's start with reframing your intention:

Intention #1: The Win-Win

Negotiation is not an act of battle; it's a process of discovery. Despite what you've been told before, your intention in a negotiation is not to win—it's to uncover enough information to *find the win-win.*

The BREW Method reframes your approach from opposition to opportunity, so you can discover a middle ground where both parties feel successful.

> **NEGOTIATION IS NOT AN ACT OF BATTLE; IT'S A PROCESS OF DISCOVERY.**

You need to move from "How do I win?" to "How do we create the best outcome for both of us?" (You can even ask your client that question directly.)

If you can enter into a negotiation with this objective in mind, you can let go of all of the battle tactics and focus on brewing a positive outcome. Negotiating is simply a structured conversation aimed at mutual success.

In fact, let's even reframe the word negotiation. Instead, let's call it a "conversation that drives performance."

When you can shift your perspective, it changes the way you frame the conversation. There's a lot of power in that change.

In trainings, I often show a picture of my dog in two different frames and ask people which they like better. They always gravitate toward one or the other. Why? Even though the picture itself is the same, the framing changes the perspective. It's no different in sales—the way you frame the conversation is everything.

You can have the same facts, the same information, even the same number goal in mind, but framing the conversation with positivity and productivity removes the conflict and paves the way for mutual success.

Intention #2: Removing Emotion

When conversations feel difficult, your emotions take over. And when emotions take over, you forget your plan. You say things you shouldn't say. You react negatively. And that win-win slips through your fingers, likely leading more to a lose-lose where everyone walks away unhappy.

Think about how you feel when you're in a conflict. Your heart rate increases. You feel tense. You get anxious. These are signs that your emotions are taking over.

Why does this happen? From a neuroscience standpoint, our brains have two operating systems: a "fast" system for automatic, emotional reactions and a "deliberate" system for thoughtful responses. When your emotions get heightened, you're in the fast system. You're going to be more confident, cool, and credible if you can move into the deliberate system. That's where you can problem solve.

Remember, *you're* the one that needs to lead the conversation. You are the one that needs to prove your credibility. And you can't do that if you get caught up in an emotional response.

That's why we *prepare*. That's why we create structure. The more that you plan, prepare, and practice, the better you can be at staying neutral and working toward a win-win.

Intention #3: Define Your Objectives

Once you've committed to your other two intentions you can focus on the business outcomes you're looking to achieve.

Start with your KPIs (key performance indicators). How will you measure whether a conversation is successful? What does success look like? Your mind probably jumps to a dollar amount here. While that dollar amount does matter, let's think beyond it.

What are you looking for from this conversation? Is it about establishing or maintaining a quality relationship, improving responsiveness, or securing future referrals? Dollars will always be a factor, but knowing your other KPIs gives you more variables to work with.

If possible, discuss these KPIs with your client before the "conversation that drives performance" and mutually agree on what success looks like.

From there, you can focus on what I call "Knowing Your Zone," meaning defining these three numbers:

- Your Target: Determine the ideal outcome you're aiming for (for example, the price on your proposal).
- Your Walk-Away Point: Know the absolute bottom line you will accept. If the deal goes below this, you must be prepared to walk away. This is your source of power.
- Your Celebration Zone (or as I like to call it, your Opa Zone—named for the Greek tradition of shouting "Opa!" and smashing a glass during a celebration): This is the flexible space between your target and your walk-away point—the area where a successful deal can be made.

Knowing Your Zone

Defining these three zones keeps you focused, structured, and aware of when it's time to walk. There will be times when there's no way to get to the Opa Zone—and you need to know when it's time to move on and keep you and the other party from wasting precious time. There will be times when you get exactly what you want. And there will be plenty of times that fall somewhere in between, where you can find mutual success for everyone involved.

Structuring a Conversation for Performance

With your intention set, you're ready to structure the conversation.

Craft Your Opening

Let's talk about how you open the discussion.

Have you ever had a conversation with a romantic partner that went south almost immediately? One of you criticized the other or started off on a negative foot, and what could have been a productive conversation turned quickly into a fight? Relationship counselor John Gottman found that the way a conversation starts can predict how it ends 96% of the time.[36] This applies to sales as well, especially negotiation. The way you start the conversation sets the stage for the interaction.

If you come in guns blazing, you're signaling a battle.

Instead, your opening should:

- Affirm the relationship
- Establish data as the foundation
- Frame the discussion as a collaboration

"I appreciate our partnership and the business we've done together. I pulled our results from the last 12 months and saw a few trends I'd like to discuss. The goal today is to understand what's behind them so we can co-build a plan that better supports your needs."

Do personalize this to your voice. But don't lose the ultimate structure. Keep your language positive and productive.

"Thanks for taking the time to talk through this. The goal today is to find a path forward that feels like a big win for both of us."

"I'm really looking forward to exploring how we can make this work for you and your team."

Setting the stage positively creates a collaborative, productive environment where you can work toward a real win-win.

---

36 Andee Tagle, "The Secret to Lasting Love Might Just Be Knowing How to Fight," *NPR*, February 24, 2024, https://www.npr.org/2024/02/24/1233730322/the-secret-to-lasting-love-might-just-be-knowing-how-to-fight.

Prepare Your Data

Prepare to use objective data, not emotions. Gather data about observable patterns that you can use to work through the conversation. (You'll learn how to use this data in the E: Engagement section.)

Prepare Curiosity-Based Questions

Next, you need to structure the questions you will ask to guide you toward your win-win. Instead of making statements use open-ended questions to gather information.

Here are some examples of the types of questions you can prepare and practice before the conversation:

- Strategy questions: Ask questions to help you dig deeper into what your client's big picture plans are. Finding out more about their strategy and their goals gives you opportunities to understand *their* KPIs and objectives, making it clearer where the middle ground win-win lies.
- Process questions: You can also ask more detailed questions about their processes, workflows, and challenges. This gives you important insight into their pain points and how you can best offer solutions.
- Value questions: These questions help you understand what they're looking for or, for existing clients, what they value about your relationship and where you can improve.

Here are some examples:

Strategy Questions	Process Questions	Value Questions
"What's changed in your book this year that I might not see in the data?" "Where are you focusing your growth efforts this quarter?" "How have market conditions affected your current strategy?"	"Where's the friction in your submission workflow?" "How has your team structure or process changed recently?" "What's working well for your team now, and what improvements are you hoping to make?"	"Where have we dropped the ball in our partnership?" "What support would help you improve [specific metric]?" "Which part of our process creates the most work for your team?"

Plan out your questions in advance and practice them out loud. Asking the right questions can lead you to the win-win.

Structure Your Close

You also need a plan for how to end the conversation, whether you end up with a win-win or not.

If the conversation ends up successful, end it with a Mutual Action Plan. Document specific agreements, assign ownership, and set timelines and success metrics. This ensures the momentum you've built continues after the meeting.

And what if the conversation is not successful? Part of your structure is knowing when and how to walk away positively if you can't find that win-win.

Keep it neutral, not emotional:

"You know, based on our conversation, it doesn't seem like we have a mutual fit right now, and that's perfectly okay. I really appreciate your time and transparency."

You also need to know where you're willing to compromise. If your walk-away point is $2,000 and the other party comes in with a ceiling of $1,850, you have three choices. You can stand firm and walk away, you can lower your price, or you can find an alternative that fits within the budget. Maybe you can adjust your original package with less features to align with their budget and still maintain your bottom line.

Knowing where you are and are not willing to work with the other person can help you reach a productive endpoint.

R: Raise Confidence in Negotiations—Managing Emotions

The biggest piece of confidence in a negotiation is knowing how to take the emotion out of the conversation.

Emotions will come up. But to be a leader, you need to learn how to move yourself from the emotional fast system to the deliberate system.

Here's how to do that:

1. Name It: Silently label your emotion: *I notice I'm feeling defensive.* Acknowledging your feelings reduces the emotional intensity and gives you back control.

2. Get Curious: Next, reframe your internal monologue. Instead of thinking, *I must win this point* shift to *I want to understand why this is coming up.*

3. The Pause: Research by neuroscientist Dr. Jill Bolte Taylor shows that it takes about 90 seconds to process emotional chemicals.[37] Giving yourself time can help your body process an emotion so you can move forward. It's okay to pause and say, "Let me think about that for a moment." This gives your "fast" brain time to cool down before you respond.

4. Take 5: After a tough conversation, take five minutes to reflect not on the outcome, but on your performance. How did you manage your emotions? Did you stick to your structure? This is about your own growth.

Of course, your physical presence matters when it comes to confidence too. Everything we covered in previous chapters about open posture, visible hands, steady eye contact signals to your own brain and to the other person that you are calm, in control, and ready to collaborate.

E: Engage in Negotiating—Working Toward the Win-Win

Now let's talk about how to put it together, engaging in the actual conversation. This comes down to two pieces: the discovery process and handling objections.

---

37 Jill Bolte Taylor, "My Stroke of Insight," TED Talk, Monterey, California, February 2008, 18 min., 48 sec., https://www.ted.com/talks/jill_bolte_taylor_my_stroke_of_insight.

The Discovery Process

The big rule of thumb here is "evidence" language over "emotional" language. Emotional language is subjective, reactive, abstract or exaggerated. ("You're always," "you never," "That's a terrible idea," "That's unreasonable.") It puts the other person in defensive mode. Evidence language, on the other hand, is neutral, factual, and non-critical.

When we "wing it," we fall into emotional language. Instead, use this SBI+I Framework to set up your evidence language:

S (Situation): Start by explaining the situation, establishing the timeline and the context:

"As we prepare for your contract renewal on December 1st, I reviewed your account usage over the last 12 months."

B (Behavior): Then, note the behaviors that you have seen—observable patterns (without judgment or your own interpretation or assumptions):

"The data shows that your team has consistently utilized about 150 support hours per month, while the current agreement is scoped for 100 hours."

I (Impact): Next, connect the behavior to the business outcome with a neutral statement:

"The impact on our end is that we've been absorbing the cost of that extra support to ensure you're covered. To continue providing that same level of service sustainably, we need to align the contract with your actual usage."

I (Interest): Finally, end by expressing genuine curiosity about the other party's impact or thoughts:

"I'm interested in discussing if this 150-hour level is the new normal for you and how we can structure the new agreement to best support that ongoing need."

This approach is data-driven. It's realistic. And it does not place blame, accuse the other party of any wrongdoing, or put them in a situation where they need to defend themselves. It's simply communicating the evidence and opening the door for a discussion that helps discover mutual success.

Here's what this looks like in action:

Brew It Better	
Instead of this…	Try this…
"I was looking at your Q3 results. It looks like your team is still ignoring the A/B testing feature we've talked about, which is why your click-through rates are 20% lower than they should be. You're leaving a lot of conversions on the table by not using the platform correctly."	Situation: "As we look toward your upcoming renewal, I've been analyzing your campaign performance from Q3." Behavior: "The data shows that 90% of your team's campaigns go live with a single ad creative without using the A/B testing feature." Impact: "We're seeing a click-through rate that's about 20% lower than our benchmark for clients who regularly test creative." Interest: "I'm interested in understanding if there are any roadblocks to using that feature and exploring if adding some dedicated strategy support in the new contract could help you capture those missed conversions."

The first example uses emotional language: ignoring, should, not using it correctly. These words are subjective and not data-based, and they can unintentionally leave the client feeling judged or criticized.

But the reframe with the SBI+I Framework leans on data, stays neutral, and opens the door for a potential upsell that benefits both parties.

Here's another example:

Brew It Better	
Instead of this…	Try this…
"I got your request for a discount. To be honest, that's not possible. Our data shows your team's usage has actually gone up by 40% this year after you added two new departments, and our costs to support you have increased as well. We won't be able to move forward with a lower price."	Situation: "Thanks for sending over your thoughts on the renewal proposal. I was just reviewing your request in the context of your account's activity over the past year." Behavior: "The data shows that your team's platform usage has actually increased by 40% year-over-year with two new departments being onboarded in the last six months." Impact: "Your team is now supporting more users and getting significantly more value from the platform, while our own support and infrastructure costs have risen to match that growth." Interest: "I'm interested in better understanding the budget constraints you're facing so we can explore how to ensure the value you're receiving continues to align fairly with the investment."

See the difference? Same facts. Different framing. The first approach is confrontational. It feels like an "us versus them." And it's more likely to lead to the client walking away than any form of win-win. It doesn't invite more discussion. It shuts it down.

The reframe leads with data, shows why a discount is clearly unreasonable, and opens the door for more conversation regarding budget.

Which one gives you more opportunity to discover valuable information? Which one shows that you value your client and yourself?

This framework takes practice. But that practice pays off. It turns negotiation into a true conversation that drives performance.

Handling Objections

The right framing sets the stage for a productive conversation. And at the same time, there will still be objections—that's inevitable.

How you handle those objections is what determines whether you end up at a win-win or not.

When you get pushback or an objection in a negotiation, your "fast" brain will immediately want to argue or get defensive. Resist that urge. An objection is simply an invitation to get more curious and re-engage the client in the discovery process.

Here are some techniques to try:

Attunement

To overcome objections, you need to get to get to the core of the other person's concern and show them that you hear and understand them. Let's define attunement: the ability to accurately notice and intepret another person's verbal and non-verbal signals in real time so they feel seen and aligned.

In his book, *Never Split the Difference: Negotiating As If Your Life Depended On It,* former FBI negotiator Chris Voss popularized several techniques that help you redirect objections.[38] Here are my favorites:

- Label: Start by naming the emotion or the issue you're hearing. This shows you're listening and builds empathy. It often starts with, "It sounds like..." or "It seems like..."

  "It sounds like pricing is a major concern."

- Mirror: Repeat the last one to three words of their statement as a question. This makes them feel heard and prompts them to elaborate on their concern:

  "You're seeing competitors come in significantly lower?"

- Question: Ask a calm, open-ended "how" or "what" question to get to the core of the issue.

  "What specific lines of business are you finding the biggest gaps?"

---

38 Chris Voss and Tahl Raz, *Never Split the Difference: Negotiating As If Your Life Depended On It* (Harper Business, 2016).

Now let's put it together. Let's say a client raised a concern about the onboarding process being difficult. Here's what this technique would look like:

Brew It Better	
Instead of this…	Try this…
"It's not complicated at all. It's actually very standard, and our clients usually find it easy once they get started."	(Label) "It sounds like the onboarding process is a real concern for you." (Mirror) "You feel that it might be too complicated?" (Question) "What specific part of the process feels like it might create the biggest hurdle for your team?"

Interests Over Positions

In any negotiation, people state a position, the specific thing they are demanding: "I need a 20% discount."

But behind every position is an underlying interest—the *why* behind their demand: "I have a strict budget I must adhere to," or "I need to prove to my boss that I got a great deal."

Instead of arguing with their position, get curious about their interest.

Brew It Better	
Instead of this…	Try this…
"We can't guarantee a specific ROI like that because there are too many variables outside of our control." "We can't do that. The premium support package is never included for free."	"I understand that a strong, measurable ROI is critical. Help me understand the goal behind that 50% number. Is it a target you need to hit for your board, or is it about ensuring the project pays for itself within a specific timeframe? What does success for this project ultimately look like for you?" "I understand that premium support is important to you. To make sure I'm on the same page, can you help me understand a bit more? Beyond the cost, what aspect of the premium support is most important for your team's success right now? Is it the 24/7 access, the dedicated manager, or something else?"

The first responses shut down the conversation. They create a stalemate with nowhere to go. See how the reframes redirect the client back into the discovery process? They invite more conversation and more information. More information means more possibilities.

Find Options

When you and your client are stuck on a single point, the conversation can feel like a dead end. You can either choose to accept the dead end or bulldoze the wall. One way to do that is exploring other options.

Instead of caving in or walking away, use "what if?" and "how?" questions to find options that might work for both of you.

"I understand the challenge with the 12-month term, and I appreciate you sharing your leadership's constraint. What if we explored some different options to bridge that gap? For example, could we structure the agreement as a 12-month contract but with a 6-month opt-out clause based on hitting certain performance metrics? Or what if we started with a more limited scope project on a 6-month term to prove the value first? How can we explore a path that gives your leadership the flexibility they need while still allowing us to form a real partnership?"

This opens the door for more collaboration without giving in to requests that aren't realistic for you.

Brew It Better	
Instead of this...	Try this...
"I'm sorry, but my absolute best and final is $9,000. I can't go any lower."	"It sounds like we're firm on our respective numbers for this specific proposal, and that's okay. What if we looked at other variables to bridge that $1,000 gap? For example, could we adjust the payment terms to be net 30 instead of net 60, which might help your cash flow? Or what if we kept the price at $9,000 but I included an extra onboarding session for your team at no charge? How could we explore making the overall package work for you?"

Obviously this approach only works with requests that are reasonably close to your win-win. If your proposal was for $9,000 and they rebut with an offer of $1,000, you probably don't have room for negotiation. This comes back to knowing your zone and understanding where you are willing to compromise.

Experiment with these techniques and see what works for you in which settings. Ultimately, remember that the goal of handling objections is to get back to the discovery process—from there, you can uncover the win-win and end with your structured close and mutual agreement plan.

W: What About _______?—When You Hit a Standoff

Negotiations rarely go in a straight line. Here's how to handle common "blanks" and standoffs.

What if...they come in hot? Let them. Don't match their energy. Acknowledge their frustration ("It sounds like you're really frustrated with this situation"), let them vent, and then gently guide the conversation back to the data and a collaborative frame.

What if...you truly can't find the middle ground? Sometimes, a deal isn't meant to be. The most powerful move a confident negotiator has is the ability to walk away gracefully. Remember, if you've explored all the options and you're at your walk-away point, it's okay to say, "Based on our conversation, it sounds like we might not have a mutual fit right now, and that's perfectly okay. I really appreciate your time and transparency." This preserves the relationship and leaves the door open for the future, proving you're not desperate.

Espresso Shot: Your Challenge

The Taco Tuesday Reframe: Your challenge this week is to identify one small, everyday negotiation in your personal life (with a partner, kid, or friend). Instead of reacting emotionally, consciously pause and think: "What's the win-win here? What information do I need to discover?" Practice reframing it from a conflict to a collaborative problem-solving moment using the techniques from this chapter.

Summary: BREW in Negotiation

B: Be the Moment (Intention & Structure)

- Your goal is NOT to win a battle. It's to discover a win-win, remove unproductive emotion, and reframe the conversation around mutual success.
- Know your zone. Before you start, define your three key numbers: your ideal Target, your absolute bottom-line Walk-Away Point, and the flexible "Opa!" Zone in between.
- Have a plan for your opening (setting a collaborative tone), your middle (preparing evidence and key discovery questions), and your close (planning for a Mutual Action Plan or a graceful exit).

R: Raise Confidence (Managing Emotion & Power)

- Manage your "fast" brain (fight or flight) reaction to conflict and consciously shift to your "deliberate," thoughtful brain.
- Have tools ready to manage emotion in the moment, like naming your feeling internally (*I notice I'm feeling defensive*) or taking a strategic pause before responding.
- Stand strong in your zone. Knowing your walk-away point is your ultimate source of power, freeing you from desperation.

E: Engage (The Discovery Process)

- Use the SBI+I Framework: Present your evidence neutrally using the Situation, Behavior, Impact, and Interest framework to state facts without placing blame.
- When you get pushback, don't argue. Re-engage them in discovery:
  » Use Label → Mirror → Question to dig deeper into their concerns.
  » Focus on their underlying Interests, not their stated positions.
  » Brainstorm and find options by introducing new variables.

W: What About _______? (When You Hit a Standoff)

- *What if...they come in hot?* Don't match their energy. Acknowledge their frustration and gently guide the conversation back to your data-driven structure.

- *What if...you truly can't find a middle ground?* Have the confidence to end the negotiation gracefully ("Based on our conversation, it doesn't sound like we have a mutual fit right now, and that's okay.").

PART 4

Find YOUR Moment

CHAPTER 16

Take a Breath, Make a Moment

Okay. Let's all just take a deep breath.

We've covered a lot. Prospecting, networking, meetings, presentations, follow-up, negotiating, frameworks, acronyms, shifts in mindset. It's easy to get to this point and feel completely overwhelmed, thinking you have to perfectly implement everything at once.

And when you do that, chances are you will end up not changing *anything* because it's too overwhelming.

The life of a salesperson is a life-long masterclass in juggling a massive amount of personalities, emotions, and dollar amounts at all times. You're answering to everyone (your manager, your clients, your ops team) while trying to continually hit a number that probably feels daunting. It can be exhausting.

So before we go any further, I want you to remember that you aren't aiming for a full overhaul. Instead, you're working on a series of 1% shifts. You are not reinventing everything you already know how to do. You are leveling it up, one small, intentional change at a time.

The goal of everything you've learned here is to help you get off the hamster wheel so your communication moves conversations forward. It's to help you feel like the leader in the room. It's to build your credibility so you can connect with confidence.

And at the end of the day, all of these strategies—every single one—boil down to a single purpose: *to create the space for real, human moments to happen.* That's the secret sauce. It's the magic in approaching sales the BREW way.

> **CREATE THE SPACE FOR REAL, HUMAN MOMENTS TO HAPPEN.**

We can get so caught up in the frameworks and the process that we forget the point. The point is the person in front of you. The point is being present enough to see them, to hear them, and to connect with them. All the structure in the world is just a tool to free up your mental energy so you can stop worrying about what to do next and simply *be in the moment.*

The magic is not in the perfectly executed cadence; it's in the genuine laugh you share with a prospect. It's not in the flawless presentation; it's in the insightful question they ask because you made them feel comfortable enough to be curious.

So as you feel the weight of all this information, let it settle. Take a breath. And with that in mind, let's move on to the next chapter and figure out where *you* should begin.

CHAPTER 17

Unpack Your Power Three

Early on in the book, I asked you to write down "My Power Three." This is where you're going to find your starting line.

Open up the note on your phone or pull out the paper where you wrote them down and recorded the ideas that jumped out to you. We're going to identify *your* three places to start.

I want you to take a moment and reflect on everything we've covered. Look over the notes you took. What resonated most deeply with you? Not what you think *should* have, but what actually *did*.

Maybe it was:

- The idea of flipping your meeting open with the ACT (Appreciate, Confirm, and Together, Set the Goal) framework
- The challenge to stop asking questions you already know the answer to
- The concept of using a through line in your presentations

- The simple reframe from "I'm sorry" to "Thank you for your patience"
- The strategy of using a time-based subject line to cut through the noise

It doesn't matter how big or small they are. What matters is that they sparked an emotional reaction in you. That's how you know they're your starting point.

Circle your top three ideas that resonated with you. These are your three things to focus on. Not the entire book. Not a complete overhaul of your entire sales process. Just these three.

Write them down. Put them on a sticky note on your computer. Make them your mantra for the next month. Practice them until they become second nature. If you struggle, start with trying to practice them in your personal life, then move into a business setting. Keep practicing. Master them. Once they feel like habit, you can come back and choose your next three.

That's how you create change for yourself. That's how you build real, lasting momentum—not by trying to do everything at once, but by making your own small moments that cascade into something bigger over time.

Remember that you can do this. You are the moment maker.

CONCLUSION
Get Brewing

When we began this journey together, you might have felt stuck or stagnant. Maybe your relationships with clients felt strong but weren't leading to the close. Maybe you were frustrated with being ghosted by clients or feeling like something was just not clicking.

My goal as you wrap up this book is for you to feel something different—you feel confident and empowered. (And don't forget to check in on your progress by taking the Connect to Close post-assessment at SalesAndPresence.com/assessment to compare you or your team to where you started. Seeing your growth and learning can foster that confidence.)

We've covered a lot of ground, moving from the simple idea that moments matter to the frameworks you can use to intentionally create them. We deconstructed what it means to have structure and intention, how to build and project real confidence, how to engage with curiosity, and how to navigate the inevitable curveballs along the way. We've brewed a new approach together.

But if you take only one thing away from this book, let it be this: selling doesn't have to feel like convincing or conquering. At its best, sales is about one thing: *human connection*.

The BREW Method, the frameworks, the 1% shifts—they are all simply tools designed to clear away the noise, the pressure, and the bad habits so you can focus on the person in front of you. They give you the structure and confidence to be truly present, listen deeply, and create moments that resonate long after the meeting has ended.

> **AT ITS BEST, SALES IS ABOUT ONE THING: HUMAN CONNECTION.**

Your journey as a moment maker doesn't end here; it's just beginning. The magic happens not in the reading, but in the doing. It happens when you consciously choose to ask a better question, truly listen to the answer, and replace a "sorry" with a "thank you." It's in the small, consistent actions, the 1% shifts, that build on each other, creating the momentum that will redefine your success. This isn't just about changing your sales numbers; it's about changing how you show up in the world with more presence, more confidence, and more connection.

Thank you for joining me on this journey. The moments are out there waiting. Now go brew some.

To your success,

—Amy

RESOURCES

For free visual resources, head to SalesAndPresence.com/resources.

Want to keep diving into the deeper learning? Register for my course at SalesAndPresence.com/course.

Ready to bring the power of moment making to your entire team? Bring me in as a speaker or trainer at AmyReczek.com/booking.

To evaluate your progress as you or your team implement the BREW Method, find our pre-assessment and post-assessment at SalesAndPresence.com/assessment.

Discover your networking profile with our quiz at SalesAndPresence.com/networking.

Need to revisit the BREW outline or some of the reframes and scripts? Find them here or at SalesAndPresence.com/BREW.

The BREW Method

B: Be the Moment—Be the moment in momentum by creating structure and intention. This is the prep phase—the way you start making moments *before* you even walk into the room or pick up the phone.

R: Raise Confidence—Power poses, nonverbal communication, how to dress, how to hold your body…this step is about commanding the room (or the Zoom call) with confidence and credibility.

E: Engage—This is where you create engagement, listen to hear instead of listening to respond, and form connections.

W: What About _______?—Let's be honest, interactions aren't always smooth. Clients push back. You forget what you were going to say.

Technology glitches. Someone you counted on doesn't show up. Embrace the awkward and use it to pivot better, listen better, and make moments in unexpected ways.

BREW in Prospecting

B: Be the Moment

- Reframe your intention. It's *not* to make an immediate sale. Your true intention is to get their interest and build familiarity/activate priming bias.
- Personalize, don't pitch. Research and identify your ideal prospect and find a way to offer them value.
- Build your cadence. Structure a sequence of at least six touchpoints, frontloaded as much as possible.

R: Raise Confidence

- Get out of your own way. Waiting a week to follow up isn't being polite; it's a sign of *your* lack of confidence.
- Reframe it. You're not trying to "sell them." You're trying to help them solve their problems.
- Practice until you become it. If making calls or sending videos feels uncomfortable, practice! Power pose before you dial. Rehearse your voicemails. Discomfort fades with practice.

E: Engage

- Call first, then email.
- Reframe your voicemails to:
  - » Acknowledge the unexpected call ("I know you weren't expecting my call...").
  - » Focus on *their* world by referencing something specific you researched.
  - » Direct them to an easy next step (like the email you're about to send).

- Keep emails concise, focus on the value you can offer *them*, and use "you framing" instead of "I framing."
- Use DMs & texts for connection first, not sales pitches. Reference a shared interest or their recent activity to open a door.
- Use video to stand out and create a powerful visual connection. Keep it brief (under 60 seconds) and authentic.

W: What About _______? (When Prospecting Hits a Wall)

- *What if...they don't respond after your full cadence?* Don't delete them or keep hammering them with the same ask. This means "no *right now*," not "no forever. Transition them from your active prospecting list to a long-term, low-touch quarterly nurture plan.

BREW in Networking

B: Be the Moment

- Remember that your intention isn't to "get clients" on the spot. It's to make three new connections, learn something new, or secure one to two follow-up conversations.
- Have a plan. Ditch the "safety nets" (running to the bar, hiding behind your phone). Set your goals before you walk in the room.
- Prep your presence: Have your nonverbal cues primed—phone away, open posture, ready to make eye contact.

R: Raise Confidence

- Stick to the plan. Your structure is your biggest confidence booster and reduces the anxiety of "winging it."
- Project openness. Use confident posture and visible hands to appear approachable and invite connection, even when you don't feel 100% comfortable.
- Have the confidence to ask questions beyond the generic "What do you do?" and to break away from the safety of your usual group.

E: Engage

- Ditch default questions and stale conversation starters. Instead, spark conversations based on the environment ("That cocktail looks interesting," "Is this your first time at this event?").
- Ask questions about what *they* care about to build a genuine relationship, not just to pass the time.
- End with a soft CTA. The goal is the next small step ("Mind if I send you that article?" or "Perhaps we could grab coffee next week?").

W: What About _______?

- *What if...you don't know anyone?* Revert to your preset goal of meeting three new people. Find someone on the edge of a group or standing alone and introduce yourself.
- *What if...the conversation lulls?* Comment on the surroundings to restart the flow.
- *What if...you're "not feeling it"?* Set a micro-goal: "I will talk to two new people, and then I can make a polite exit."

BREW in Meetings

B: Be the Moment

- The ACT opening: Structure your opening to grab attention.
  - » Appreciate their time
  - » Confirm the timeframe
  - » Together, set the goal (focused on *their* desired outcome)
- The GUIDE conversation framework: Structure the middle of the meeting to guide the discovery process from context and pain to business impact and solutions.
  - » Gather context with fact-finding questions (ones you *don't* already know the answer to)
  - » Understand needs. Uncover the pain point, and keep asking questions

- » Identify the impact. Don't jump to your solution. Keep digging to find out why the pain point really matters.
- » Demonstrate understanding. Repeat what they said back to them, using their words.
- » Offer empathetic solutions. Resist the temptation to skip to the pitch.

- The REPS closing framework: Structure your close for clear momentum.
  - » Recap key points.
  - » Explore any missed items.
  - » Outline the plan of action (your steps + timeline, their steps + timeline).
  - » Set the next meeting.

R: Raise Confidence

- Use confidence from Control: Your structural frameworks (ACT, GUIDE, REPS) eliminate uncertainty and boost your confidence as the meeting leader.
- Focus on your nonverbal cues: Use confident meeting posture (leaning in slightly), keep hands visible on the table, and make eye contact with everyone in the room to project leadership.

E: Engage

- Listen to understand, not to respond: Practice the "power of the pause" after someone speaks to truly hear them, not just to plan your own response.
- Ask impact questions: Don't just stop at identifying a pain point. Engage them on its business consequences: "What is the tangible *impact* of that on your team?"
- Speak with empathy: When offering a solution, first acknowledge their feeling or the impact of their problem ("Wow, it sounds like that issue is causing a lot of stress...").

W: What About _______?

- *What if...someone hijacks the agenda?* Acknowledge their point, suggest a separate discussion ("park it"), and gently guide the conversation back to the agreed-upon goal.
- *What if...you're asked a question you can't answer?* Don't bluff. Confidently state you will find the correct information and follow up by a specific, promised time.
- *What if...someone is disengaged?* Avoid calling them out. If necessary, gently re-engage them with a direct question that values their expertise ("Sarah, I'd be interested in your perspective on this").

BREW *in Presentations*

B: Be the Moment

- Find your through line. Identify a single word or theme (e.g., "connection," "simplicity") that connects all your points and weave it throughout.
- Plan an engagement tactic for the first 60 seconds (question, poll, show of hands).
- Plan your transitions. Know how you'll bridge from one slide to the next without just reading the title.
- Structure your close to be a concise recap built around your through line.

R: Raise Confidence

- Ground yourself with anchors. Before you start, remind yourself of three to five core, non-work truths about yourself to anchor your confidence in your inherent worth.
- Remember the rule of three for eye contact. Don't scan the crowd. Plan to make genuine eye contact with just three friendly faces in different parts of the room.

- Own the stage physically. Use open, confident posture. For an advanced move, start off-stage and walk through the audience as you begin.

E: Engage

- Lead the slides; don't let them lead you.
- Incorporate movement or activity where you can (even virtually).
- Adjust your energy and pacing based on the audience's real-time feedback.

W: What About _______?

- *What if...the tech fails?* Acknowledge it with grace. Be prepared enough with your core message to continue without slides if necessary.
- *What if...someone is disengaged?* Ignore them. Focus your energy and eye contact on the people who *are* leaning in.

BREW *in Follow-Up*

B: Be the Moment

- Reframe your intention. You're there to add value and move the conversation forward to a clear next step.
- Use two different types of cadences:
  - » New connections: A fast, condensed sequence of touchpoints (call, email, social) within the first week to maintain momentum.
  - » Existing clients/nurture: A slower (monthly/quarterly) cadence focused on providing consistent, non-salesy value.
- Investigate before re-engaging: If a prospect has gone silent ("ghosted"), figure out what you might have missed in previous interactions before reaching out.

R: Raise Confidence

- Center yourself on the value you're offering.
- Let go of self-doubt and have the confidence to execute your planned sequence without second-guessing every step.
- Depersonalize silence. Reframe their silence as being about *their* priorities, not a personal rejection of you. This detaches your ego and prevents desperation.

E: Engage

- Ban "just checking in" and "following up on" from your vocabulary.
- When re-engaging a silent prospect, lead with a human touch, reference *their* specific pain points from your last conversation, and propose a clear CTA
- Use curiosity-driven subject lines: Apply the principle of using time/dates (e.g., "Wednesday, May 10th") to create FOMO and get your email opened.
- Stick to value. For nurture follow-ups, send articles, podcasts, or insights related to *their* interests, not just your product features.

W: What About _______?

- *What if...they still don't respond after your re-engagement attempts?* Respect their silence. This is a clear "no, not now." Gracefully transition them to your long-term, low-touch nurture list. The active pursuit is over for now.
- *What if...they reply with "Now's not a good time"?* Maintain control by proposing a future check-in. "Completely understand. I'll plan to circle back around the start of next quarter. All the best until then."

BREW *in Negotiation*

B: Be the Moment

- Your goal is NOT to win a battle. It's to discover a win-win, remove unproductive emotion, and reframe the conversation around mutual success.
- Know your zone. Before you start, define your three key numbers: your ideal Target, your absolute bottom-line Walk-Away Point, and the flexible "Opa!" Zone in between.
- Have a plan for your opening (setting a collaborative tone), your middle (preparing evidence and key discovery questions), and your close (planning for a Mutual Action Plan or a graceful exit).

R: Raise Confidence

- Manage your "fast" brain (fight or flight) reaction to conflict and consciously shift to your "deliberate," thoughtful brain.
- Have tools ready to manage emotion in the moment, like naming your feeling internally (*I notice I'm feeling defensive*) or taking a strategic pause before responding.
- Stand strong in your zone. Knowing your walk-away point is your ultimate source of power, freeing you from desperation.

E: Engage

- Use the SBI+I Framework: Present your evidence neutrally using the Situation, Behavior, Impact, and Interest framework to state facts without placing blame.
- When you get pushback, don't argue. Re-engage them in discovery:
  » Use Label → Mirror → Question to dig deeper into their concerns.
  » Focus on their underlying Interests, not their stated positions.
  » Brainstorm and find options by introducing new variables.

W: What About _______?

- *What if...they come in hot?* Don't match their energy. Acknowledge their frustration and gently guide the conversation back to your data-driven structure.
- *What if...you truly can't find a middle ground?* Have the confidence to end the negotiation gracefully ("Based on our conversation, it doesn't sound like we have a mutual fit right now, and that's okay.").

ABOUT THE AUTHOR

Amy Reczek, keynote speaker, founder of Sales & Presence, and author of *So, You're in Sales…* spent 17 years in the corporate sales trenches watching talented people get stuck in outdated, energy-draining tactics. She knew there had to be a better way.

So she built one.

Amy founded Sales & Presence to challenge the traditional sales playbook and replace it with something far more powerful: authentic confidence, psychological awareness, and the ability to turn everyday conversations into moments that create real momentum. With a background in psychology and a certification in nonverbal communication, she doesn't just teach sales strategies—she teaches the science and art of human connection.

Today, Amy works with teams and organizations around the world, helping them stop "selling" and start truly connecting. Through her speaking, training, and writing, she equips professionals with the skills to show up with presence, clarity, and impact.

When she's not working, Amy enjoys drinking coffee, traveling, and spending time with her husband and two dogs. Her next dream venture is to own a sanctuary farm for animals.

ACKNOWLEDGEMENTS

There's so much more that goes into writing a book than you can ever imagine until you do it. In a lot of ways, it's just like sales, communication, and connection, and for that matter, just like brewing a cup of coffee. We see the finished product: the book, the close, the delicious cup of life fuel. We don't see all the nuances that make it possible. In sales, it's everything in this book: the structure, the intention, the confidence, the verbal and nonverbal communication. In coffee, it's whatever goes on inside the machine: the water flowing through the pipes, heated to the exact perfect temperature, extracting the beans (to trace it back further, it's the way the plant is grown and harvested). And in writing, it's everything that takes one little idea through to the final book you're holding in your hand or reading on your screen.

I'd like to take a moment to shine a light on some of the people who helped do that for me.

First, thank you to my husband, who stood by my side when I was writing a book while running and growing a company, all while we navigated a move from Colorado to California without even having our new home set up. It was an adventure, and I'm glad you were there to take it with me.

Thank you to my team at Sales & Presence for all of your work to support the business and keep us moving forward.

I'd also like to acknowledge the many of you who showed me how to look at sales in a different light. Your support gave me the confidence to form the ideas that eventually became the BREW Method, and this book wouldn't be possible without you.

Thank you to the editing team for finessing and refining this book and keeping my spelling errors in check. I appreciate all of your insight and hard work.

Finally, thank you to coffee. Sweet, wonderful, coffee. Without you, I wouldn't have made it.

And thank you, readers, for taking this journey with me. Now get out there and brew your own ideas in the world!

—Amy